Confident Coding

*Learn how to code
and master the essentials*

THIRD EDITION

Rob Percival and Darren Woods

KoganPage

First published in Great Britain and the United States in 2017 by Kogan Page Limited
Second edition 2020
Third edition 2023

2nd Floor, 45 Gee Street
London
EC1V 3RS
United Kingdom

122 W 27th Street
New York, NY 10001
USA

4737/23 Ansari Road
Daryaganj
New Delhi 110002
India

© Rob Percival and Darren Woods 2020, 2023

ISBNs

Hardback   978 1 3986 1189 4
Paperback   978 1 3986 1188 7
Ebook   978 1 3986 1190 0

British Library Cataloguing-in-Publication Data

A CIP record for this book is available from the British Library.

Library of Congress Control Number

2020941863

Typeset by Integra Software Services, Pondicherry
Print production managed by Jellyfish
Printed and bound in Great Britain by CPI Group (UK) Ltd, Croydon CR0 4YY

Confident Coding

Contents

Introduction

The train drew into the platform on that cold, wet and dreary morning. The greyness of the day sat well with the monotony of my regular commute, a one-hour train journey from Cambridge to London. I had a functional job – it paid the bills without being particularly challenging and my colleagues were friendly enough – but it just lacked inspiration for me. A humble enough man, I was contemplative yet grateful. This position had been my gateway into employment after a less than stellar higher education showing. It was a job of processes, of administrative tasks, which once mastered simply occupied my time rather than challenged any mental agility or incited engagement.

As the rain lashed down and the raindrops careered down the glass pane I glanced out of the window and made out the pillar across the tracks. I'd observed it a thousand times, Victorian brick, well-weathered but with an impermeable scrawl of graffiti emblazoned across the breastwork. I'd often read the messaging aloud in my head, perhaps arrogantly dismissive of the seemingly clumsy language used. But this morning would be different. Those words were to be prophetic. I can't explain why, but for the first time I stopped to contemplate their meaning.

"If not now, when?"

It was an epiphany to say the least. Until that moment, I'd had no clear plan, structure or even drive, just a haphazard collection of vague thoughts and an attitude of one day, one day my time will come... I'll do it then.

Suddenly I knew what I wanted to do, what I needed to do. The clarity of thought was liberating, the rush of enthusiasm that I felt surge through me invigorating. That very morning, I picked up a coding book from the bookshop on the walk to the office and I was coding up my first website into the evening.

The next day in work I was actively seeking out those laborious tasks and thinking of ways in which I could automate them. By midday I was creating a macro in Excel and then tweaking its code in Visual Basic for Applications (VBA). Then I discovered Microsoft Office Access and its very accessible database and form features. Before I knew it I was automating processes and handling the data for my team, saving me and my colleagues time with robust and efficient use of software tools. My efforts and new-found skillset didn't go unnoticed for long. Perhaps appreciative of the series of dynamic reports which were now being generated in real time, my manager granted me a promotion to a more specialized, IT-focused role and so the ball began to roll.

Fast forward some 20 years and I love working for myself as a self-employed programmer; I contribute on a multitude of projects across many different sectors and engage with a wide community of professionals. I enjoy the flexibility and freedom to determine my own work commitments and I manage a great work–life balance. But perhaps most importantly of all, I continue to be motivated and engaged by the empowerment that coding affords.

I don't think you ever lose that spark, which is the thrill of problem solving and learning, evolving and adapting new skills.

The most important thing for you to realize right now is that this is all achievable for you as well. Picking up and reading these first pages is hopefully a good beginning, but please indulge us and read on. It's up to you how far you wish to take coding and your career. Whether you are just enhancing your current skillset and job role or planning the next entrepreneurial software platform, all it takes is a bit of a down payment in terms of time and commitment and the horizon is yours.

Learning in-demand skills

In October 2019, BBC News published an article entitled 'Vatican launches new eRosary bracelet'. The article went on to discuss the new bracelet, which enabled users to connect to the 'Click to Pray eRosary' app. The app, it reported, provided a track of progress and aimed to fulfil the purpose of the traditional rosary in aiding prayer and meditation. The technical achievements of the bracelet aside, it's amazing to observe how far technology has permeated into and become prevalent in everyday society. Here we have one of the oldest and most famous institutions of the world, steeped in tradition and history, venturing forth with exciting and innovative gadgetry. The eRosary bracelet is a sophisticated, stylish and contemporary piece of technology, replete with online connectivity and services, aiming to complement the user's lifestyle and faith needs.

This illustrates what we already know: the world is ever changing; the thirst for technological advancement and its application strive forward at great pace. Beneath the shiny exterior of our modern lifestyles and connected services is the hard work and programming skills of many dedicated professionals, at all levels. There is ever increasing demand for skilled coders – but this demand is not limited to pure programming roles. Dentists, lawyers, police officers, etc, with complimentary coding knowledge are sought after for workplaces across the globe. Like a foreign language, and even more universal, coding skills have become a huge asset to possesses on any résumé.

Then there's the money side of things: the research firm Burning Glass found that jobs requiring coding skills pay, on average, $22,000 more, and that half of all jobs with salaries over $58,000 require some coding skills. Moreover, half of all programming opportunities were in industries outside of technology, including finance, manufacturing and healthcare. Learning to code not only makes a candidate more employable, but also gives them the freedom of starting their own business, or creating a side income from making websites and apps.

In this book we will look in detail at both the 'why' and the 'how' of learning to code: after looking at the benefits that programming knowledge brings, we will dive right in to learning HTML, the language of all websites. We will then look at a range of other programming languages, and even see how to build native apps for iPhones and Android devices.

Finally, we will apply the skills in step-by-step guides to entrepreneurship, building your own websites and apps, increasing your everyday efficiency and even seeing how you might become a full-time software developer. Even if you have no plans to change careers, we will see how you can use coding skills to make yourself and your colleagues more efficient, creating shortcuts to complete tasks faster, provide quicker feedback and serve your customers and clients better. Our hope for you in reading this book is that you will become fully digitally literate. Some of you may go on to create businesses; you may build an app to help you in your current job; and you might communicate more effectively with the IT team at the office. But most importantly, you will have a greater understanding of how coding underpins every interaction we have with our computers, our phones and our smart devices. The lines of code that you write will enable you to better harness the technology that you use every day.

Who are we?

Rob Percival

I would like to take a moment to tell you how learning to code has changed my life. I studied Mathematics at university, and went on to become a teacher in a secondary school in London. I very much enjoyed the teaching, but I suspected it might not be what I wanted to do for my whole life, so in the evenings and weekends I started to build websites.

I had done a little coding as a kid, trying to replicate my favourite computer games on a BBC Micro, but I was certainly no Mark Zuckerberg or Bill Gates. I would simply have an idea for a website, and using Google figure out how to put it together. This method of learning was free and fairly effective, but it did mean that I often went down long, unnecessary detours until I discovered that there was a much better way of doing things.

My first website was HomesExchange.org, a site that allowed people to swap homes for a couple of weeks to save accommodation costs. Unfortunately, I hadn't realized that the domain name HomesExchange.org could also be interpreted as HomeSexChange.org. After a few unsavoury support requests, I decided the business was unlikely to go very far!

I built several more sites, most of which came to nothing, until one day I came up with the idea of an eco-friendly web hosting service, to allow people to host their websites and emails in an environmentally friendly way. This was an example of *scratching my own itch,* as I had looked for such a service myself for my own sites, and the existing options were generally very expensive and didn't have as many features as the big web hosts like GoDaddy and 123-reg.

The service, ecowebhosting.co.uk, turned out to be something that a lot of people wanted, and it started to grow quite naturally, as people discovered the website through Google and word-of-mouth. As the site grew in popularity, I added features and automated processes that I had to do several times a day, learning the coding required as I went.

In 2012 I quit my teaching job in order to focus on Eco Web Hosting and some other projects full time. I quickly discovered that working freelance is not quite as 'freeing' as I thought, as I always had several activities going on at once. I liked having a range of reliable income (through the web hosting), new projects (mostly freelance websites and apps through local contacts) and starting new businesses when I had the latest 'great' idea. But I was also struggling to cope with so many competing calls for my attention.

In January 2014 I started to build an online course to teach people how to build websites. I had noticed that online video courses were becoming popular, and thought that with a combination of my coding knowledge, teaching skills and entrepreneurial experience I might be able to offer a fun, practical and project-based approach to learning to code. That course, The Complete Web Developer Course, went on to be one of the best-selling courses of all time, and I followed it up with The Complete iOS Developer Course, for iPhone apps, and The Complete Android Developer Course, for Android apps.

Through my courses, I have now taught over half a million people how to code, and I daily appreciate the scale that the internet can provide, with one person being able to help so many others. The courses have also brought me financial freedom, and a strong desire to continue helping others find the joy that coding brings me, as well as the many opportunities that learning to code brings.

Steve Jobs famously said, 'I think everybody in this country should learn how to program a computer because it teaches you how to think.' That is a final, and essential, benefit – learning code forces you to approach problems logically and analytically, asking the right questions and testing your solutions to see if they work. And that is a skill that will benefit you in all aspects of your life.

Darren Woods

Much like Rob, coding has had a profound impact on my career and life. Starting out working in a school in the administration office, I quickly started to realize how inefficient certain tasks and procedures were. This wasn't a reflection of the hard work of the team, it was just the inherent nature of some of the processes required. So, I set out on a mission (admittedly, in the first instance, to make my life easier) to improve the efficiency of the administration of the school. It was in this moment that I realized the potential of IT to deliver the desired benefits.

At first improvements amounted to applying obvious off-the-shelf software solutions. But I soon began to realize the big gains were achieved when I started to become interested in coding and customizing software for specific needs. Starting off by coding Excel macros and Access on the school Microsoft Office software, I caught the bug. Before long, I was borrowing books from the library and studying online tutorials and steadily increasing my skill set.

Coding was a great enabler for me. With my newfound confidence and skills, I started to think how I could apply these in various other environments. It was obvious being able to code opened a huge range of opportunities across almost every industry and field of work.

Before long, I'd gathered my portfolio together, bought a new suit, hired some office space and suddenly, I was running my very own software development company. I've never looked back; coding has been a revelation and a seismic change in my career and the opportunities it has afforded me. I would encourage you to simply explore the opportunities open to you through learning to code... where it takes you from there is up to you.

How to use this book

This book is designed to be as practical and hands-on as possible. You'll get the most out of it by actively taking part and following every instruction and activity online as we go.

There are three different kinds of features in this book to help you learn coding: questions, practice exercises and challenges. The quick questions are designed to help you memorize key pieces of information, the practice exercises make sure that your new skills are honed and developed, and the challenges stretch you to deeper learning. As the book progresses, you'll find that there are fewer quick questions but more and more challenges.

We will be using the context of a Visitor Registration application – something that may well be useful in a huge range of different businesses. Of course, it will be baby steps at first; but at each stage, we want you to free your thinking. For each exercise and technique you meet, we encourage you to experiment and extend to improve your results, perhaps tailoring it to your specific professional environment or incubated prototype idea. When we introduce our real-life requirements as a context to our learning, we acquire knowledge and skills very effectively.

I hope you enjoy the journey!

Supporting material online

From time to time in the book we'll be pointing you to supporting material online. Here's how to get it.

1 In the book each online resource is keyed with the letters CC and a number – like this: **CC21**
2 Go to koganpage.com/cc
3 There you'll see a 'View resources' button.
4 The button takes you to a PDF, 'Online material'.
5 The PDF gives you the corresponding URL for each CC number.

There is another PDF you can download from the same location, koganpage.com/cc. '*Confident Coding* images' contains all the images in the book so you can enlarge them on screen.

PART ONE

Why coding?

## CHAPTER ONE

Why coding is important and what it can do for you

We've already seen several reasons why learning to code is important: it can increase your salary, widen your future career choices and be a springboard into self-employment and entrepreneurship. It will also help you navigate the increasingly automated future of smart assistants, self-driving cars and virtual reality.

In this chapter we will look at some more specific things you can do with coding right now, many of which we will expand on through the course of this book.

Becoming more efficient

Almost all jobs today require a fair bit of time working with a computer. You likely have to do a range of similar tasks each day, including working with email, creating and managing documents, and searching the web. Almost all of these tasks can be made more efficient with a strong knowledge of how the software and operating system you are using work.

Initially, simply using keyboard shortcuts will likely save you several minutes each day, and more importantly will start you thinking about how the software you are using works, and how your workflow could be improved. Services such as text expansion and If This Then That, which we will be covering in detail later on, can save you a huge amount of time, as well as helping you do a better job. Imagine being able to automatically email your colleagues with a summary of the effectiveness of your weekly newsletter. Or completely automating the process of turning your weekly sales report into a live webpage that your colleagues can view any time.

Learning to code will allow you to do all this and much more, doing a better job in less time.

Communicating with technical people

Regardless of your current fluency with technology, it is likely that you need to communicate with technical people fairly regularly about things that you don't entirely understand. Whether it is trying to get some content added to the company website, getting some software installed on your computer or removing the tweet you accidentally posted on the company account, greater technical knowledge can make every aspect of those conversations much more straightforward.

As well as becoming more familiar with the terminology that technical people use (which really isn't as complicated or mysterious as it seems), you will know the fundamental nature of how computer systems work and fit together. This means that every time you come across a new system, or piece of software, you will be able to zero in on the key functions and properties, enabling you to get to grips with how it works, and discuss it confidently.

Being secure in your ability to deal with computers and software will dramatically improve both your productivity and your speed with which you can get things done when working with technical staff in your company.

Understanding how software works

One of the primary reasons programming is being taught to young children is because of the speed with which the world of software develops. Our current primary computing device, the smartphone, has only been around in its current form for 10 years. Who knows what devices we will be using 5, 10 or 20 years from now? Teaching children to code teaches them the fundamentals of how software works, which are not likely to change any time soon. This will enable them to quickly adapt to new operating systems, different programs or apps, and new devices.

The same is true for adults – learning how computers work gives you the power to absorb new software and hardware into your workflow, making you more adaptable and essentially future-proofing your career.

Knowing what it takes

Further to understanding how software works, learning to code gives you an awareness of what is involved in building a webform, or adding a feature to an app. It is likely at some point in your career that you will need to work directly with coders to add features to the company website, customize the software you use every day, or even to create a new app from scratch.

If you aren't aware of what is necessary to build a website, app or individual feature, you are open to either overpaying for what you are getting, or not getting exactly what you wanted. Knowing what it takes to write some code gives you power in negotiations and while managing a project, as well as the ability to get the job done quickly and to budget.

Building your own website or app

Before the internet, if you wanted to share an idea, product or service with the world, there were significant obstacles to over-come. You would have had to publish information in a newspaper or book, or sell directly through shops. The web changed all that, and now you can build a website in a matter of hours which is immediately accessible to the 3 billion people currently online. The only obstacle is learning to code.

To me that is a hugely exciting concept – coding enables you to build the equivalent of a worldwide shopfront with nothing but a laptop and a (free) text editor. No more bricks and mortar required.

We'll look at several different ways to build your own website and app (and why you might want to) throughout this book.

Building a web presence

Eighty per cent of employers Google job applicants before invit-ing them for interview. Take a moment to search your own name and see what comes up. Is it what you would want a potential employer to see? Creating a blog, portfolio site, or a simple site for a project you've undertaken or ebook you have written enables you to control what your future boss sees, and helps you stand out as an applicant.

A web presence matters and learning to control yours will put you ahead of 95 per cent of the population. We will cover the whys and hows of the creation of blogs and portfolio sites later on in this book.

Starting your own business

'Technical cofounders', ie people who want to start a business, and have coding skills, are so highly in demand that whole websites have been dedicated to the task, and the search phrase 'find a technical cofounder' has 3.2 million results on Google.

Coding skills enable you to start any business you like, but they also enable you to partner with people and provide the technical expertise that all new companies need. Whether or not you want to start a company today, knowing that the opportunity is always there is incredibly exciting, and we will look at the process in some detail later in this book. What entrepreneurial opportunities could learning to code bring you?

Taking on extra responsibilities within your current role

In many jobs there is not an obvious process for advancement. Or perhaps there is a process but it is a slow one, and you are looking for opportunities to speed up your next promotion. It can be difficult to simply 'do your job better', or find other ways to stand out from the crowd.

Learning to code gives you the ability to, for example, build an app that makes something that you and your colleagues do regularly easier or more effective. You could create a webpage that helps people to arrange car sharing, or if you are a lawyer you could build an app to allow clients to instantly view the status of their case, and be automatically alerted to any updates. Or you could simply take responsibility for your area of the company website, making sure it is up to date and perhaps introducing tools and features that become popular with your customers or clients.

Doing things like this might sound extraneous or unnecessary, but they will get you noticed, and can be the beginning of something big. Even if they are not, you will learn a huge amount building your idea, and make lots of mistakes, which, with any luck, you won't make next time round.

Aim to stop 'selling your time'

Through employment, most of us earn our income by selling our time. If you love your job, that's a perfectly reasonable arrangement, but for many of us the opportunity to 'scale up' what we do would be welcome. Learning to code can provide that opportunity.

If you are a teacher, create a website teaching people your subject, and sell advertising space. If you are an artist, create an app showcasing your work and selling prints. If you are an accountant, create a tool that simplifies your workflow and offer it to others for a small fee. We will take you step by step through the process of creating something that people want later in the book, but start thinking about it now and jotting down ideas whenever you can.

Combine coding with your professional expertise

Most full-time coders have only ever worked as developers. If you have a different professional background, combining that with coding can create something close to magic.

For me, it was the combination of coding and teaching that worked so well, but for you it might be coding and law, coding and accountancy, or coding and yoga (we'll see an example for that later on). Being an expert in a separate field lets you know what people like you want, what problems they have, and gives you insight into how those problems might be solved. Learning to code gives you the tools to actually solve them.

Coding is fun

Coding can be a huge amount of fun, and very satisfying as you overcome problems and complete challenges. You may feel that you are not learning anything new in your day-to-day role, and learning to code gives you that buzz of acquiring new skills and understanding that you may not have felt since school or university.

If you enjoy problem solving and creating things, you will likely find great enjoyment in completing a project, fixing bugs and creating websites and apps. Crafting lines of code to get a computer to do your bidding is addictive in itself, and a wonderful break from the stress of everyday life.

Coding and specific industries

Hopefully the above has given you ideas of how you could use coding skills in your current role, but if not here are a few concrete examples of how programming could improve your prospects in specific industries.

Law

Technology is becoming increasingly central in every industry. Knowing how to code as a lawyer or accountant gives you an edge with technical clients, enabling you to speak their language and see more clearly where they are coming from. Not only that, but technology often pushes the law forward, forcing it to adapt to new possibilities and unforeseen situations. A sound grasp of the technologies themselves is a huge advantage in a fast-changing legal landscape.

Legal practices also increasingly rely on technologies such as apps and websites for everyday office tasks, and the ability to streamline these processes can make you far more effective and efficient. You may also be able to please your clients better: the legal process can often seem slow and frustrating to both individuals and companies. Creating tools for them to see both what is happening and what they need to do in real time could set your practice apart.

Sales and marketing

Sales and marketing have been absolutely transformed by technology. The ability of marketers to measure the effect of their campaigns has changed the landscape entirely, and being comfortable with the latest technologies can set individual marketers and salespeople apart. Whether that's through being able to write, edit and debug the HTML for your email marketing campaigns or automating repetitive tasks to free up your and your teammates' time to develop innovative new ideas.

Even working with 'old media' can be made vastly more efficient and effective when combined with technology, and if the tool doesn't exist for you to properly manage your latest campaign, coding skills give you the power to create it.

Banking

It goes without saying that technology is at the centre of banking today. Machines can make trades far quicker than humans can, and consumers are increasingly interacting with their banks online and through apps. Whatever your position in the banking sector, understanding the tools that you and your colleagues use every day enables you to use them more effectively.

If you spend all day in Excel creating financial models, learning to code can not only help with the process of finding bugs in your formulas and check your results, but can also give you more powerful techniques to automate processes you are currently doing by hand.

Trade industries

While the actual processes of building houses and fixing boilers are still the role of humans, a strong grasp of technology can still give people working in trade industries an edge. Customer service is an important aspect of any tradesperson's role, and being able to swiftly reply to queries, arrange appointments automatically, and manage invoicing and payments efficiently will not only save time but result in a much happier customer base, and more repeat business.

As with other sectors, if you create a tool that solves a problem for you, it is very likely others will be interested in using it too, and you will be perfectly placed to market your product or service to people in your industry.

Creative industries

As a photographer, graphic artist or other creative professional, it is likely that you are already focused on technology, and are an advanced user of a range of complex software. But it is also likely that you find yourself doing the same processes repeatedly: exporting to various file types and sizes, applying filters, tweaking colour values and much more. Being able to automate some of these processes can both make you more efficient and give your output a more consistent style.

It is also inevitable that you will work with developers, perhaps to create your own portfolio site, or working together on a particular project. Being able to communicate effectively with them is crucial for a job to go well, and once you get to the level that you can build your own websites or apps, you can offer a more complete service to your clients.

Retail and service

The retail and service industries are all about providing a great experience for your customers. That often means providing a great digital experience that is more efficient for both the organization and the end-user. Having command of that technology and being able to create and customize features for your users is highly attractive to employers, and enables you to do a better job day-to-day.

Summary

These are just some of the very practical ways that learning to code can improve your prospects, make you more valuable as an employee and give your opportunities for greater freedom and career advancement. As Jason Calacanis, CEO of Mahalo and founder of the start-up showcase LAUNCH conference says, 'An employee who understands how to code is valued at about $500,000 to $1 million toward the total acquisition price.' That's a lot of value to create by learning a new skill.

We will look in more detail at all of these opportunities later in this book, once we have learned the coding languages that they require. Before that, however, we will spend a little time demystifying coding. We will learn what exactly coding is, why there are so many coding languages and which ones you should learn. We'll also see how both the internet and offline apps function, and familiarize you with the basic terminology that you will come across in this book (and in all those conversations with technical people that you are about to have).

On a final, more general note, we have found that learning to code gives people a great feeling of empowerment. Having the ability to create digital products such as apps and websites is something very few people can do, and brings so much potential into your life. It has completely changed our lives, and it can do the same for you.

## CHAPTER TWO

What coding is

For people who haven't programmed before, coding can feel like a mysterious art. The mythical 'coder' is someone who (usually while wearing headphones, hoodie and supping carbonated beverages) can coax a computer into doing their bidding by typing frantically on a keyboard or two. In reality, the whole process is much more straightforward than that.

In this chapter, we will explore what programming is and write the first few simple lines of code for our Visitor Registration application. We'll also look at the different types of software we can produce with code, including websites, mobile apps and programs for desktop computers. Finally, we will learn some general coding processes that will stand you in good stead before we tackle our first coding language, HTML, in the next section.

What is coding?

Put simply, coding is the process of writing lines of instructions that make a computer (or tablet, or phone, or watch) do something. But it's a little more complicated than that, so let's cover a little bit of background.

The fundamental electrical component that allows a computer to do what it does is the *transistor* – a tiny piece of electronics that can either be *on* (ie allow electricity to pass through) or *off* (electricity cannot pass through). Current computer processors have around 2 billion transistors, which can turn on and off around 3 billion times every second. (Incidentally, *Homo sapiens* has 100 billion neurons which can turn on and off about 1,000 times a second, so we're getting quite close to being able to simulate the power of a human brain.)

What this means is that computers 'think' in a series of 1s and 0s, with 1 meaning 'on', or true, and 0 meaning 'off', or false. In the very early days of computing, the only way to communicate with a computer was to enter streams of 1s and 0s, but this of course wasn't very practical. So gradually computer 'languages' were developed, which allowed people to give the computer instructions in a more convenient way.

A computer language is much like a human language such as English or Spanish, in the sense that each language has specific commands (words) and syntax (punctuation), so both the human and the computer can understand it. However, a key difference between computer languages and human languages is that computer languages are absolutely precise and unambiguous. If you spell a command incorrectly, or forget a semicolon, it is likely that your whole code will fail. Unlike a human conversation, computers are extremely fussy about both spelling and punctuation.

The big advantage of this unambiguity is that you can be certain that if you get your code right the computer will do exactly what you want. Unlike human conversation, which can often result in unexpected outcomes, computers will always do exactly what is commanded of them.

But I can control a computer without coding

You might be thinking, 'but I can do everything I need to with my computer and phone without needing to code.' In the last 30 years or so highly user-friendly operating systems such as Windows and MacOS (and Android and iOS on mobile devices) have meant that we no longer have to write code to control a computer. Advanced Graphical User Interfaces (GUIs) have been developed so that anyone could approach a computer or phone and start using it straight away. This has been a great leap forward in usability, but it also means that many people aren't aware of the power that they have at their fingertips if they go beyond the everyday software like Word and Chrome.

Every piece of software you use has been written, in code, by someone or, more likely, a group of people. Every time you issue an instruction to Siri, or enter a web address in a browser, a few (or a few thousand) lines of code are executed to answer your question or load a website. There is no magic behind this, it is simply the hard graft of thousands of developers and billions of transistors doing what they are told.

Learning to code gives you complete power over these transistors – you can bend them to your will by creating your own software, or automating processes to save you hours every day. Coding is very much like a super-power, in that it enables you to use equipment you already have in a whole new way.

Let's write some code

Let's get started with our Visitor Registration app. In your browser, go to the web address https://repl.it/languages/python3.

This website allows us to write code in a computer language called Python (we'll see more about individual coding languages later in this chapter). It will then *compile* the code for us (essentially, turn it into 0s and 1s so that the compute can understand it), run it, and then display the output for us to see.

For our application, the first thing we want our visitor to see is a friendly welcome message, instructing our guest what to do.

In the main window, type the following code:

```
print("Welcome, please register your visit here.")
```

Now press the 'run' button to compile and run your code.

You should see the phrase 'Welcome, please register your visit here.' appear in the black box at the right of the screen. Success! Now try misspelling 'print' or removing one of the brackets. If you run the code now, you will get an error, something like:

```
NameError: name 'prin' is not defined
```

This should give you an idea of how precise you need to be – the computer won't make a 'best guess' about what you meant. Let that be your first lesson! The output in the black box on the right of the screen will provide detail about the error and point you in the right direction to fix your code.

Do bear in mind, coding is a creative process as much as a scientific one, so don't be discouraged by mistakes you make as you go along. Rather, be encouraged that fixing the errors that occur is all part of a strong learning process. Think of coding just like learning a foreign language or any other new skill; it's only once we start to put techniques into practice and see how things work that we embed and cement that knowledge.

Time to try something a little more complicated. Let us suppose that, upon greeting our guest, we want our Visitor Registration application to display the car parking bay numbers that are available. Have a look at the following code, and try to predict what it will do:

```
for x in range(1, 11):
    print(x)
```

Now delete your print statement and replace it with the above code. If you get an error, check the code you have entered very carefully – you need to copy the code exactly.

Note: the print command is indented using the tab key. If you type the first line correctly and then press enter, the website should know that you want to indent the second line, so will do it for you automatically. If it doesn't, press the tab key on your computer to indent it.

Did it do what you expected? The 'for' command begins something called a 'loop', which executes a chunk of code several times. The x is a variable, which represents a value, in this case a number. The 'range(1, 11)' part runs the loop with x being 1, 2, 3, ... up to 10 (perhaps surprisingly, the 11 is not included in this command). Finally, the 'print(x)' part prints the value of the variable x. So, the output is simply the numbers 1 to 10.

Challenge 1

For the purposes of our application, let's assume that parking bays 1–9 in the office car park are reserved for employees. This leaves bays 10–20 to display to our visitor. Can you change the above code, so it prints the correct parking bay numbers?

Solution: You should have changed the code to this:

```
for x in range(10, 21):
    print(x)
```

If you did that, congratulations!

Printing the numbers like this might seem a long way off from building the next Uber or WhatsApp, but it's where all coders begin, and the same principles and techniques apply even when building complex software.

Why are there so many programming languages?

A common question for new coders is what programming language to learn, which leads to the question of why there are so many. With human languages, the many languages we speak have developed over many thousands of years within different geographical communities. With computer languages, their development was more deliberate, which means that the different languages are designed for different purposes. You don't need to become an expert in every language, and some great coders really only know one language well, but you should be aware of the different contexts that languages operate.

We will cover this in more detail later on, but for now there are broadly three types of software that you will create with code. The first we will call apps. Apps have their code stored on a device (usually a computer, phone or tablet), and primarily run on that device. An app might be Excel, or a mail client, or a browser like Firefox. It could be a game like Angry Birds, or utility such as the Notes app on your phone. Apps are what most people mean when they talk about software, and they are the simplest to understand.

Next we have the code that displays a website. This is generally not stored on your machine, and is downloaded afresh every time you load the website. The browser (itself an app, such as Chrome, Safari or Firefox) downloads and processes the code to show you the website. This is known as *client-side* code because it is processed on the client computer or phone, ie your device.

Finally, we have code that runs on a server, or *server-side* code. A server is like a very powerful computer that is always connected to the internet. Your email is stored on a server, as is your Twitter feed and the current state of your Words With Friends games. When you log into a website, you send the username and password to the server, which then runs some server-side code to check if the login details are right, and if so returns the appropriate page. If not, it will give you an error message.

For each of these three types of software there are a range of languages we can use. Please don't feel you have to know the names of all of these languages; you will become more familiar with most of them as you go through this book, but it is useful to be aware of the most popular languages in each category.

Languages for building apps

Apps are generally designed for one particular platform. That platform might be Windows, or MacOS, or Linux for desktops and laptops, or iOS (for iPhones and iPads) and Android (for Android phones and tablets). There are other platforms but these are by far the most popular.

The mobile platforms each have languages that they are designed for. iOS development was traditionally done in a language called Objective-C, but in 2014 Apple introduced a new language called Swift, which is becoming more popular, and is what we use in this book. For Android, a language called Java (note Java is not related to JavaScript) is used by default. It is possible to use other languages, but not recommended for beginners.

On Windows, most programs are written in C++, which is related to Objective-C (both are derived from an early programming language simply known as C). Some apps are written using a platform called .NET, which mostly uses a language called C#, another variant of C. There are a greater range of other development tools and languages for Windows than there are for the mobile platforms. You can use Java and Python, among other languages, to build Windows programs.

On MacOS, as with iOS, the default languages are Objective-C and Swift. Because of its open nature, you can use almost any language, including Java, Python, and two other popular languages, Perl and Ruby, to build Linux applications.

Because most new developers are keen to make mobile apps, we will be focusing on Android and iOS development (so Java and Swift) in this book, but it is relatively easy to move from those to other languages if you wish.

Client-side languages

If you are building websites, there are three core languages that you will need to control how the site looks and behaves. The first is HTML, or Hypertext Markup Language, which is what controls the content of a site. The second is CSS, or Cascading Style Sheets, which determines the styles, such as fonts, colours and layouts. The third is JavaScript, which allows your website to be dynamic, and change the content and styles based on user interaction. These three languages are inescapable in client-side, or 'front-end', development, and they are the three languages that we will start with in this book.

Server-side languages

By far the most popular language for website server-side (also known as 'backend') code is PHP, short for Hypertext Pre-processor. This currently powers around 80 per cent of websites, but there are other options. Python is also used, as is a language called Ruby. You can also use Perl, Java and even Swift to write server software.

Phew! That's a lot of languages, and you don't need to remember all these names. If you are still wondering which language to learn, it depends on what you want to do. If you want to build websites, HTML, CSS and JavaScript are crucial.

For the backend, we would recommend Python first (as it is a very easy language to learn), and PHP if you find it necessary. If you want to learn mobile development, Swift for iOS and Java for Android are your best bets.

If you have no idea what you want to do with coding at this point, simply follow along with the book and we will teach you a range of languages so you can choose where you want to focus your attention when you have finished.

Summary

You now have a good overview of what coding is for and the range of different languages and platforms available. It's time we delved in a bit deeper with our Visitor Registration application and made use of some of these technologies to bring it to life.

In the next section we will be looking at the three main languages for front-end web development, HTML, CSS and JavaScript, and one for the backend, Python. This will give you a great grounding in a range of different programming styles and techniques, and give you the power to create and manage your own websites.

PART TWO

Languages

## CHAPTER THREE

HTML

In this chapter, we'll start our coding journey by looking at HTML, the language of the web. By the end of the chapter, you will know:

- what HTML is and where it is used;
- how to update and maintain simple websites;
- how to edit HTML in a text editor, and see the results immediately in a browser; and
- how to use basic HTML elements, including:
  - paragraphs and headers;
  - lists and images;
  - forms and tables.

Along the way we will be using our new-found HTML skills to build a frontend webpage for our Visitor Registration application. This will be the welcome page when the visitor first enters our company's premises, perhaps presented on a touch screen display or tablet at reception.

What is HTML?

HTML stands for Hypertext Markup Language, and it is the language that all websites are written in. *Hypertext* describes the fact that an HTML page can contain links to other HTML pages, which was one of the founding principles behind the web.

HTML was created by Sir Tim Berners-Lee in the late 1980s as he was developing what is now known as the internet. He created it as a way of organizing his own notes, but soon wanted to share his documents with others. As the web grew, Berners-Lee's language worked so well that others adopted it for adding formatting to text, forms, images, and of course links.

One aspect behind the success of HTML (as with all the languages in this book) is that Berners-Lee made it freely available for anyone to use. It is this freedom that allowed the web to grow so fast, and allows anyone today to use the same tools as professionals at no cost whatsoever. Thank you Tim!

Why learn HTML?

Strictly speaking, HTML is not a coding language, but a markup language. This means that with HTML you can change the content and layout of a website, but you are limited in terms of interactivity with users (so you couldn't build Twitter with just HTML).

This makes HTML a great place to start your coding journey because it is fairly easy to understand, and you can apply the skills you learn straight away by building simple websites, or making changes to websites you own or manage. If you find an error on the company website, you can just fix it yourself, without having to bother the IT department.

Later on in this book we will see how to combine HTML with JavaScript to start building interactivity into your pages.

What software do I need?

For this whole book, you only need to download one piece of software, and that is a text editor. This allows you to create and edit code in any programming language.

You can use any text editor you like, but we would recommend downloading Brackets from www.brackets.io. It is free and open-source, and can be downloaded on Windows, Mac and Linux. It will automatically highlight and indent your code, making writing HTML a much more pleasant experience.

I've downloaded Brackets – what now?

Once you have installed Brackets, you will be presented with this screen (3.2):

3.2

Brackets creates an HTML file called index.html, which we will use to become familiar with the basics of HTML before we start writing our own code.

You can see what this HTML file looks like in your browser by clicking File → Live Preview. This will open up the HTML file in your default browser, which will look something like this (3.3):

3.3

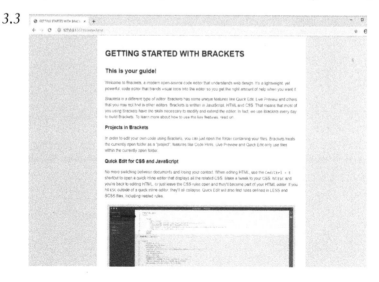

While coding, we always recommend having the text editor (Brackets) and your browser open at the same time, so that you can view changes as you make them.

This will be most effective if you position the live preview and the brackets code windows adjacent to each other; one above the other, or side by side.

Now for the fun part – try removing the '!' at the end of 'This is your guide!' in the Brackets window. You should see the live preview page update immediately, like this (3.4):

3.4

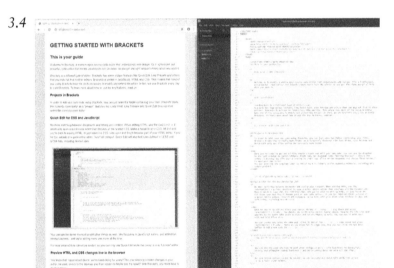

Well done, that was your first HTML edit. Feel free to spend a couple of minutes experimenting with changing the code, to see what effect that has on the webpage itself (don't worry if you mess anything up – you can always use ctrl-z (or cmd-z on a Mac) to undo your changes).

Now it's time to look in more detail at the HTML code and what it is doing. All the HTML commands come inside angled brackets (< and >), and they tell the browser how to format and display the HTML document. Everything inside the angled brackets is known as a *tag*. Let's look in more detail at the default HTML document created for us by Brackets (3.5):

3.5

The code starts with the line:

```
<!DOCTYPE html>
```

This is a standard command that tells the browser that this is an HTML document, and to process it accordingly. We put that at the beginning of every HTML document we create.

Then we have the <html> tag. This indicates the start of our html code. If you scroll down to the very bottom of the document you will see a matching </html> tag. The / here means 'end of', so </html> means that the html section of our code has ended.

Next comes <head>. This is the 'header' of our HTML document, and contains information about the document such as its title, a description and the character set (a name for the collection of letters, numbers and symbols that we are using, in this case UTF-8). It also contains a link to a style sheet, which we'll be looking at in the next chapter.

Quick question: Where does the <head> section end?
Answer: Where it says </head>

After the header section, we have the <body> tag, which indicates the beginning of the main section of our HTML. This is where we will put all the content for our webpage. Inside this section are a number of different tags, which we will be looking at in more detail shortly. Two key tags are:

- <h1> – this is a major heading. You can see in the browser window that this text is big and bold. There are a number of different heading sizes, which you can use by changing *h1* to *h2, h3* etc.

Quick question: Experiment with changing the <h1> tag to other heading sizes. How many different heading sizes are there?
Answer: 6 (h7, h8 etc just display as normal text)

- <p> – this is a paragraph tag, and is used to contain normal text. Successive paragraphs are separated by a small gap on the webpage.

And that's it. Other than learning new tags, that is everything you need to know about how an HTML page works. We start by defining the document as an HTML file with <!DOCTYPE html> then we enclose our HTML in <html> and </html> tags. Within those tags we have two sections: <head>, which contains information about the webpage such as its title and description, and <body>, which contains the content of the page.

Now that we know how an HTML page works, we're going to build our own from scratch.

Challenge 1: Our Visitor Application webpage

The best way to learn to code is by doing, so you are now going to create our application's webpage from scratch. Have a final glance over the code in Brackets to remember the key details and then press ctrl-A (cmd-A on a Mac) to select it all, and then press delete to clear the file.

LANGUAGES

Now for the challenge. From memory, if possible, create an HTML document with a title of 'Coding Solution Enterprises' (you don't need to give it a description, or define the character set), and content of 'Welcome to Coding Solutions Enterprises' inside paragraph tags. How about a second paragraph? Something like 'Please register your visit using this application.' Good luck!

Your final webpage should look something like this (3.6):

3.6

```
<!DOCTYPE html>
<html>
    <head>
        <title>CODING SOLUTIONS ENTERPRISES</title>
    </head>
    <body>
        <p>Welcome to Coding Solutions Enterprises</p>
```

```
        <p>Please register your visit using this
application.</p>
    </body>
</html>
```

GENERAL PRACTICE EXERCISES

1   Add the missing opening and closing tags to correct the HTML
    here: [CC 1]
2   Create a header and paragraph tags here: [CC 2]
3   Create three different types of header tag here: [CC 3]

Formatting text

Now that you know how a basic HTML page works, we're
going to look at some specific tags that we can use to customize
the way our page appears. Let's start with text formatting.

Try typing the following code under the 'Please register your
visit using this application'. paragraph in Brackets:

```
<p><strong>Important: Please have your license plate and
parking bay number ready.</strong></p>
```

The strong tag makes the text appear bold.

*Question: Move the strong tags around so that only the word
'Important' is in bold.*
Answer: <p><strong>Important:</strong> Please have your license
plate and parking bay number ready.</p>

Now add a new paragraph using this code:

```
<p><em>(Parking bay numbers are displayed on signs next
to each bay.)</em></p>
```

The 'em' tag is short for emphasis, and makes text appear italic.

This can act as a handy reference for basic formatting HTML tags.

Note – you might want to save that code as a separate file on your computer called formatting.html so you can refer back to it later.

Question: Experiment by adding paragraphs which contain <sup>, <sub> and <del> tags. What effect do these have on your text?
Answer: <sup> makes text superscript (ie appearing above the normal text), <sub> is subscript (ie appearing below the normal text) and <del> has a strikethrough effect.

You should end up with a webpage that looks something like this (3.7):

3.7

GENERAL PRACTICE EXERCISE

Add formatting to the text here:

HTML lists

We are now going to look at a number of more advanced HTML tags, starting with lists. Firstly, let's remove those strikethrough, subscript and superscript experimental lines we put in above. We'll also remove the paragraph in italics '(Parking bay numbers are displayed on signs next to each bay)'. Now that's done, we want to make the information required for visitor registration a bit clearer. So, change the wording of this line: 'Please have your license plate and parking bay number ready.' to 'Please have the following information ready:'. Once done we are ready for our list of items, type in the following code:

```
<ul>
      <li>License Plate</li>
      <li>Parking Bay Number</li>
      <li>Name of Person You Are Visiting</li>
</ul>
```

The <ul> tag is short for 'unordered list', and the <li> tags are 'list items'. This creates a bullet point list that looks like this:

- License Plate
- Parking Bay Number
- Name of Person You Are Visiting

Question: Try changing 'ul' to 'ol' in the above code. What effect does this have? What do you think 'ol' stands for?

Answer: ol stands for 'ordered list' and makes the list appear numbered, like this:

1 License Plate
2 Parking Bay Number
3 Name of Person You Are Visiting

<ul> and <ol> tags are useful ways of displaying lists of information. See them in action in the great 'List of lists of lists' Wikipedia page at https://en.wikipedia.org/wiki/List_of_lists_of_lists.

Side note – viewing the HTML of any website

In your browser, try loading https://en.wikipedia.org/wiki/List_of_lists_of_lists. Then right click on the website and select 'View Page Source' or similar. You'll likely see something like this (*3.8*):

3.8

This might look like mostly gobbledygook but if you look closely you'll see some of the HTML elements we have talked about: <html>, <head>, <title> etc. If you scroll down (about line 61 at the time of writing), you'll see a collection of <ul> elements with <li>. Try to match these up with the content of the page itself. Viewing them side by side gives us this (3.9):

3.9

You should be able to see how the <ul> and <li> elements in the code on the right match up with the various lists in the page itself on the left.

Try doing this with a few other websites to get an idea of how HTML code relates to a website itself. www.example.com is a nice simple one to start with, but you can try any website you like. (Warning: the code for www.google.com is not recommended at this point – check it out and you'll see why!)

Images

Adding images to webpages is very simple, and it introduces us to a new HTML concept – *attributes*. These are bits of information added to a tag that give the browser more information on how to display it. For example, to display an image, we would use something like this:

```
<img src="image.jpg">
```

The <img> tag is short for image, and the 'src' part inside is short for source. Essentially we are telling the browser where to get the image file from to display it. Notice also that <img> is a *self-closing tag* – we don't need a </img> tag to end it – it ends itself.

Question: Try putting the code <img src="image.jpg"> into our HTML file. What happens, and why?
Answer: You'll likely get a broken image symbol. This is because the 'image.jpg' file doesn't exist, so the browser can't display it.

Try replacing the above code with this. Don't worry if it looks a little large at this stage:

```
<img src="http://completewebdevelopercourse.com/
star.png">
```

As long as you have internet access and there aren't any typos in your code, you should now see this (*3.10*):

3.10

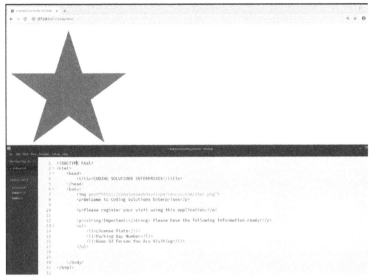

Congratulations, you've just added an image to your webpage. The http:// at the beginning of the link means we are getting the image from the internet, so we don't even need to save it to our computer.

You've probably noticed that the image is a little large in size, but not to worry: we can customize the image further by adding height and width attributes. Try putting this code into brackets:

```
<img src="http://completewebdevelopercourse.com/star.
png" height=100 width=100>
```

This will give you something like this (3.11):

3.11

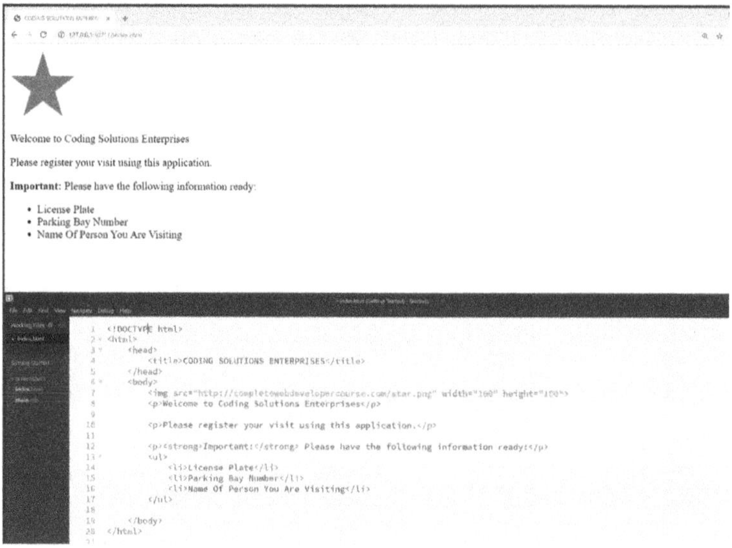

The star image is now 100 pixels wide and 100 pixels high.

Question: What code would display the image 'sun.png' with a height of 250 pixels and width of 200 pixels?
Answer: <img src="sun.png" height=250 width=200>

PRACTICE EXERCISE

Add and resize an image here: **CC 5**

Now that you are familiar with attributes and self-closing tags, we'll move on to a more complicated and powerful aspect of HTML – forms.

Forms

Forms are all over the web, and they are a simple but effective way to make your website interactive and allow your users to enter information. We are going to make use of a form on our application's webpage to allow our visitor to enter the information we require.

Text boxes

Text boxes allow the user to enter some text, such as a username or a password.

Start by entering the code below our list of required items and seeing what you get:

```
<input type="text">
```

Try typing some text into the box. It should look like this (*3.12*):

3.12

Question: What is the name and value of the attribute in this input tag?
Answer: The name of the attribute is 'type' and its value is 'text'.

This gives you a simple text input that the user can click on and type some text into. We are going to use text inputs to capture the information we require from the visitor.

Question: What happens when you change the input type to 'password'?

Answer: Try the code <input type="password">. *It looks the same, but when the user types in the box, their input is hidden. Perfect for passwords!*

Checkboxes

We can add several other form element types using the input tag. Try adding this code just above the text input we placed in the code above:

```
<input type="checkbox">Do you have a vehicle?
```

This gives the visitor an option to indicate that they have a vehicle with them.

3.13

Radio buttons

If we were to add additional check boxes, each would be independent; that is, you could check as many as you wished. If, instead, you only want your users to select one option from a group you can use the *radio* input type:

```
<p>What type of vehicle is it?</p>
        <input type="radio" name="size">Saloon
        <input type="radio" name="size">SUV
        <input type="radio" name="size">Hatchback
```

If you try out that code, you'll see that you can only select one of the options. Also, once you have selected an option, you cannot deselect it – so you *have* to choose one and only one of the options.

PRACTICE EXERCISE

For each of the following, state whether you would use a checkbox or a radio button:

1 Asking a user whether they want to subscribe to a newsletter.

2 Asking a user whether they prefer tea or coffee.

3 Asking a user what countries they have travelled to from a list.

Answers

1 Checkbox – they can select or deselect the box as they wish.

2 Radio – they should only be able to select one option.

3 Checkbox – they can then select as many as they want to (or none).

Drop-down menus

If you want to create a drop-down list where the user can select from a range of options, you can use the *select* element. It looks like this:

```
<select>
    <option>1</option>
    <option>2</option>
    <option>3</option>
</select>
```

Try this out in our webpage – let's ask the user to select a parking bay number – you should see something like this (*3.14*):

3.14

This code is a little more complicated than the input elements, but still fairly straightforward. The <select> tag introduces the drop-down menu, and then we add an <option> tag for each of the options within the drop-down.

Question: What does the </option> tag do?
Answer: It signals the end of that option, ready for us to add another one, or use </select> to end the drop-down menu.

Text areas

What about the person our visitor is coming to see? We'll need to capture as much information as possible so that we can identify the person. Therefore, we are going to need more than a little box. That's where text areas come in. You add them like this:

```
<p>Who are you visiting?</p>
    <textarea></textarea>
```

Try it out, and you'll see a larger box where you can add multi-line text. Unlike inputs, text area tags are not self-closing, so you need to add a </textarea> afterwards to end the element.

PRACTICE EXERCISE

Change the width and height of a text area using the cols and rows attributes. Create a text area that is about half the height and width of your browser window.

After a bit of experimentation, your code should look something like:

```
<textarea cols="50" rows="8"></textarea>
```

This will give you a text area that looks like this (*3.15*):

3.15

Buttons

Every form needs a submit button. You can add one by using the input type 'submit', like this:

```
<input type="submit">
```

That gives you a simple submit button with the word 'Submit'. If you want to change the text on the button, you can add a value attribute, like this:

```
<input type="submit" value="Confirm">
```

This is as far as we are going to go with forms at this point (but we will see them again in Chapter 6). They are a very simple way to allow interaction with your users, and if you are creating or editing websites, you will likely come across them before long.

Challenge 2

You know now all the basic form elements, so in a new file try creating a simple sign-up form that allows the user to enter an email address, password, and perhaps their gender. Don't forget the submit button.

PRACTICE EXERCISE

The HTML for this form is broken – can you fix it? [CC 6]

Tables

You've probably already spotted the flaw in our genius plan. We're relying too much on the user to input accurate information in that textarea. Likely, we will receive all sorts, eg Bazza, Big Dave, 'that girl with brown hair'. It would be useful if we could display people to the visitor for them to choose from. Tables are a great way of displaying information to the user – essentially they look like spreadsheets, with different content in each cell. Let's remove our textarea element and create a table. Use the following code:

```
<table>
    <tr>
        <th>Name</th>
        <th>Role</th>
    </tr>
    <tr>
```

```
        <td>Rob</td>
        <td>Director</td>
    </tr>
</table>
```

The <table> tag is pretty self-explanatory – it indicates that we want to display a table. <tr> is short for 'table row', and defines the beginning of a new row in our table. <th> is short for 'table header', so each of these is a one-column header for our table.

After the table headers, we use </tr> to signify the end of the first row, and another <tr> to start a new row. <td> is short for 'table data' and is how we refer to the content of a cell in our table. Each row should have the same number of columns (in this case 2).

Try typing that into your text editor and seeing how it looks. You should see something like this (*3.16*):

3.16

You can see that the table cells are nicely lined up with each other, and that the table headers are in bold. Voila – our first table!

Question: Add one more row to your table representing another member of staff.
Answer: Your HTML should look something like this:

```
<table>
    <tr>
        <th>Name</th>
        <th>Role</th>
    </tr>
    <tr>
        <td>Rob</td>
        <td>Director</td>
    </tr>
    <tr>
        <td>Darren</td>
        <td>Underling</td>
    </tr>
</table>
```

We can customize our tables in a number of ways. Firstly, we can change the width of the columns just like we did with images earlier:

```
<table>
    <tr>
        <th width="200">Name</th>
        <th width="300">Role</th>
```

```
        </tr>
        <tr>
            <td>Rob</td>
            <td>Director</td>
        </tr>
        <tr>
            <td>Darren</td>
            <td>Underling</td>
        </tr>
    </table>
```

3.17

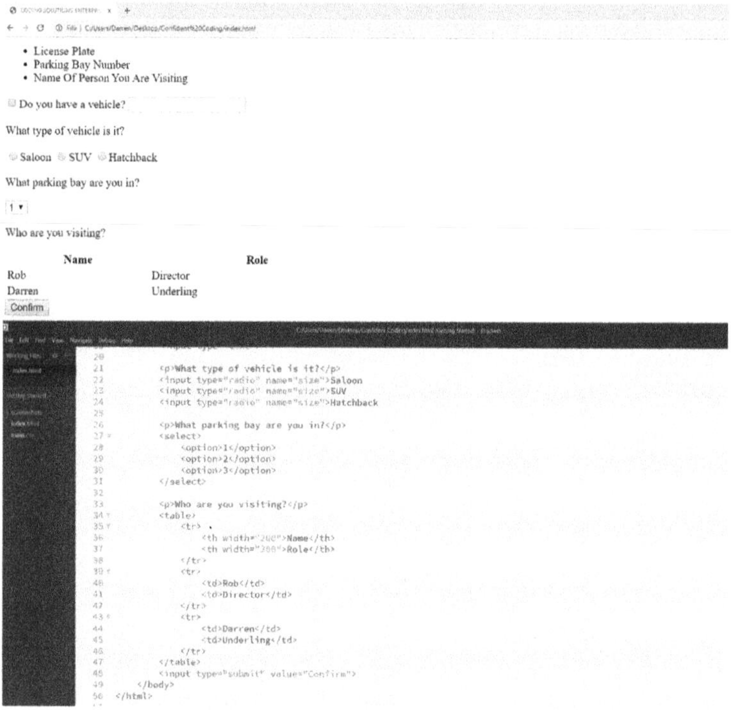

Notice that when we do this the table headers are centred, but the table data is left-aligned.

We can also add a border around the table cells by adding the attribute border=1 to the table element (*3.18*):

3.18

Challenge 3

Create a table with 'First Name' and 'Surname' as two separate table head labels and your actual first name and surname in separate table data cells in the table body: CC7

Links

As we mentioned at the beginning of this chapter, the 'HT' in HTML stands for *Hypertext,* which refers to HTML's ability to link to other webpages. Insert the following paragraph and link into our webpage. Let's put it just under the text 'Please register your visit using this application.' so that it is one of the first things our visitor is prompted to do.

```
<p>Please read the following information:</p>
    <a href="http://www.hse.gov.uk/workers/index.
htm">Health and Safety in the Workplace</a>
```

The 'a' element is actually short for 'anchor', because links were originally used to link from one part of the page to another part, the location of which was defined by an 'anchor' (we'll see how to do that shortly). 'href' is short for hypertext reference, and is essentially the page that we want to link to. The Health and Safety in the Workplace text that appears inside the 'a' element is the text that the user will click on to go to the new page.

Try this out, and you'll see your text is underlined and blue, and when you click on it you are taken to http://www.hse.gov.uk/workers/index.htm (*3.19*):

3.19

(You can click the back button in your browser to go back to your webpage.)

Question: What happens when you add target=_blank as an attribute to the <a> element?

Answer: Your code should look like this:

```
<a href="http://www.hse.gov.uk/workers/index.htm"
target="_blank">Health and Safety in the Workplace</a>
```

When you click on the link you should find that it opens the link in a new tab or browser window.

Anchor links (ie links within a webpage) work slightly differently. Firstly, go to the bottom of our page and add the following:

```
<p>Code of Conduct</p>
```

```
<p>Lorem ipsum dolor sit amet, consectetur adipiscing
elit. Sed cursus dictum sem. Praesent volutpat accumsan
felis vitae gravida. Aliquam ex elit, mattis vel ipsum
sit amet, auctor varius dolor. Mauris sed eros
consectetur, fringilla nisl quis, bibendum ex. Proin
sit amet rhoncus metus. Duis convallis pulvinar orci ac
ultricies. Vestibulum bibendum velit a dui laoreet
efficitur. Sed lobortis suscipit sapien eget pharetra.
In feugiat iaculis turpis id ornare. Proin volutpat
eleifend est, eu cursus massa faucibus ut. In in neque
lacus. Aenean nec ante ex. Maecenas fermentum posuere
arcu, nec venenatis est euismod semper. Ut congue et
sem et tincidunt.</p>
```

We've used placeholder text for the second paragraph here, but you can find something a bit more in context for your own company (3.20):

3.20

Now, give the Code of Conduct paragraph on the page an id attribute, like this:

```
<p id="conduct">Code of Conduct</p>
```

(We'll be seeing a lot more of the id attribute in the CSS chapter.)

Finally, change the code for the link at the top to look like this:

```
<a href="#conduct">Code of Conduct</a>
```

The # (hash) symbol tells the browser that instead of jumping to another page, it should look for an id tag of 'conduct' in the current page and jump there.

Try it out. This type of link will only jump to the content if is currently off-screen. If you have a large screen and you can already see the full page, you might need to make your browser window smaller so that you need to scroll to see the code of conduct then click on the link. You should find when you click on the link it jumps to the bottom of the page.

PRACTICE EXERCISE

Practise creating links in the exercise at (**CC 8**)

HTML entities

Sometimes you might want to use symbols in your webpages, such as the copyright symbol ©, the euro symbol € or even a smiley face ☺. This can be done by using *HTML entities,* or special codes that browsers display as the required symbols. So to display a trade mark we use:

```
&#8482;
```

Let's place a trademark immediately after the text of our company's name in our welcome message (*3.21*):

3.21

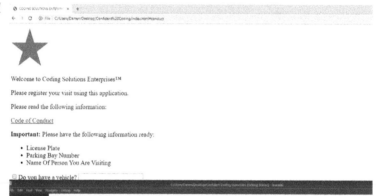

The & tells the browser that we are about to enter an HTML entity, and the # indicates we are going to describe the entity by its code number. The code number for the trade mark sign is 8482, and then we use a semicolon to complete the HTML entity.

Some symbols can be displayed using a code number and also a code name, so:

```
&copy; and &#169;
```

will both display the copyright symbol ©.

You can see a list of some of the most common HTML entities at www.w3schools.com/html/html_entities.asp

Challenge 4

Try using HTML entities to add currency symbols here: [CC 9]

iFrames

This is the final bit of HTML we will be learning in this chapter, so congratulations for making it this far. Soon we'll be seeing how to add some style to our application's webpage using CSS.

iFrames allow us to include the content of another webpage in our own. So, for example, we could include the health and safety page we saw earlier at the bottom of our webpage using this code:

```
<iframe src="http://www.hse.gov.uk/workers/index.htm">
</iframe>
```

3.22

Try changing www.example.com to other websites that you visit, such as bbc.co.uk. Note that some popular websites, such as google.com and facebook.com, don't allow their websites to be displayed in iFrames.

Question: Can you add some attributes to the <iframe> element to make the iFrame box as wide and tall as your browser window? Answer: Just add width and height attributes as we did with images:

```
<iframe width="600" height="500" src="http://www.hse.
gov.uk/workers/index.htm"></iframe>
```

This will give you something like this (3.23):

3.23

One particularly handy use of iFrames is to include media such as YouTube videos in your webpages. For our application you could imagine embedding a company help video posted to YouTube or perhaps a promotional piece about the company's achievements as part of the overall welcome message. To do this:

- Go to youtube.com and click on any video you like.
- Scroll down and click on the Share button (underneath the red Subscribe button).
- Click on Embed.
- Copy the code to your clipboard (ctrl-c or cmd-c on a Mac) and then paste it into your webpage. You should end up with something like this (*3.24*):

3.24

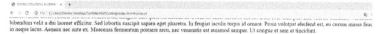

The code is a simple iFrame with a width and a height, but also has the attributes *frameborder="0"*, which turns off the iFrame border, and *allowfullscreen*, which is a YouTube-specific attribute that, as you might have guessed, allows the user to make the video full screen.

PRACTICE EXERCISE

Try adding an iFrame to include any website you like here: CC 10

Summary

As we have learned, HTML forms the basis of every webpage. You have now learned how to create and edit all the foundational HTML elements. You should feel confident with the progress we have made on our application's webpage and be able to apply that learning to creating your own webpage or editing an existing one.

The next step on our coding journey is to learn how to style our HTML pages – we will look to improve our Visitor Registration webpage by adding colour, changing sizes, adjusting text formatting and a lot more. We do that using CSS, or Cascading Style Sheets, and that's what we'll be looking at in the next chapter.

Further learning

At this point of the book, we would recommend going on to learn CSS and JavaScript before investigating HTML further. However, if you have got the HTML bug, feel free to check out these resources to dive deeper into how the language works and what you can do with it:

- www.codecademy.com/courses/web-beginner-en-HZA3b/0/1 (archived at https://perma.cc/CSF2-D2UH) – interactive coding exercises for HTML.
- www.w3schools.com/html/ (archived at https://perma.cc/J6YW-Q2RR) – free HTML tutorials.
- http://learn.shayhowe.com/html-css/ (archived at https://perma.cc/NV65-FCUG) – great site for learning HTML and CSS.
- https://play.google.com/store/apps/details?id=com.sololearn.htmltrial&hl=en (archived at https://perma.cc/H4LH-FWQJ) – free Android app for learning HTML.
- https://itunes.apple.com/gb/app/learn-html-fundamentals/id933957050?mt=8 (archived at https://perma.cc/GEV4-QZJ3) – free iPhone and iPad app for learning HTML.

## CHAPTER FOUR

CSS

Now that you have covered HTML, which allows you to create different types of elements on a webpage, in this chapter you'll learn how to style those elements using CSS. Then, in the next chapter, we'll be making the elements interactive using JavaScript.

In this chapter we'll cover:

- what CSS is and how it is used;
- how to refer to elements using classes and IDs;
- using DIVs to break up our webpage; and
- how to use CSS to adjust the following:
  - borders and positioning;
  - colours and fonts;
  - text and link formatting.

What is CSS?

HTML allows us to add elements to our webpages, but it does not easily allow us to adjust their position, colour, font or style in general.

CSS was introduced by Håkon Wium Lie, a colleague of Berners-Lee, in 1994. The main idea is to keep the styling information separate from the content of the page, so it's easy to adjust the style without affecting the content. In fact, you can completely change the look and layout of a webpage by just changing the CSS, without editing the HTML at all.

CSS stands for *Cascading Style Sheets* – the 'cascading' part refers to the way the browser decides which style 'rule' should apply to an element when there are multiple, conflicting rules. For example, if one style sheet says a <p> element should be blue, and another says it should be red, we need to have a consistent way to know what colour the <p> element should actually be. We'll see several examples of this later on.

Why learn CSS?

Learning HTML without CSS is a bit like learning to paint in black and white: you can draw anything you like, but you are missing out on a world of colour. CSS allows us to design our websites to look unique, friendly and pretty. It will allow you to customize the look of any website you want to build or maintain.

From a coding point of view, CSS's use of classes and IDs (we'll see what they are very soon) is fundamental to JavaScript, and will teach you how we can use a single line of code to affect the look of a number of different elements. CSS is still pretty simple, but is slightly more complex than HTML to get your head around, so it's the perfect second language to learn as you develop your coding skills.

What does CSS look like?

Enough introduction! Let's see some CSS in action and apply it to our Visitor Registration application. We're sure you'll agree our current opening webpage is presently looking a little cluttered and disjointed.

First off let's add the corporate colour to that welcome message to make it stand out a bit more. To begin with, let's change that welcome text to Heading 2 (<h2> tag). Next add a 'style' attribute, with a value of 'color:red' to the welcome paragraph so that it looks like this:

```
<h2 style="color:red">Welcome to Coding Solutions
Enterprises&#8482;</h2>
```

Through the wonder of CSS, you'll see that the text turns red. Try experimenting with other colours.

Note to our British readers: you will have to use the American spelling of the word 'color', as the British spelling colour:blue will not work.

The 'color:red' part is the CSS, and is a single CSS rule which applies to that particular <p> element.

Adding CSS using a 'style' attribute is known as *inline CSS*, as it is in line with the HTML.

There is a problem with inline CSS though – if we want to make the text of every paragraph red, we have to add a style attribute to each paragraph. This is messy, and if we suddenly want to change the colour of all our paragraphs to green, we will have to update each one individually.

Fortunately, there is a solution to this problem, and it is called *internal CSS*.

What is internal CSS?

Internal CSS is when we include all the CSS together at the beginning of our HTML document (we will meet the third and final type of CSS, external CSS, at the end of the chapter). Remove the inline style that you just made in the previous task. Next add the following code into our <head> section:

```
<style>
h2{
color: red;
}
</style>
```

Your view should now look like the below (*4.1*). Notice that although we have removed the inline style the <h1> text is still

4.1

red because of the inline CSS we've just put in. Essentially this inline CSS says 'find all the <h2> elements and change the text colour to red'. The curly brackets { and } contain all the rules that we want to apply to our h2 elements (the semicolon signals the end of a rule). Now if we want to change all our Heading 2 (h2) elements from red to green we can do so just by changing the CSS – we don't have to go anywhere near the HTML.

PRACTICE EXERCISES

1 Black text can be a little stark. Try changing the paragraph colour to a softer grey. You should see that all paragraphs are change to grey when you introduce the rule into the CSS.
   Your code should be something like this (4.2):

4.2

2 Change the styling in the webpage on this exercise link from inline to internal CSS: [CC 11]

3 Experiment with applying CSS rules to other elements within our webpage. Try to choose styles that complement each other and contribute to making the page readable.

Your code should look something like this (4.3):

4.3

Classes and IDs

What if we wanted some paragraph tags to be blue and others red? We need a way to select elements more precisely than just by their type. We do this using classes and IDs.

Classes

Adding a class attribute to an element is simple – change the code for the first paragraph to make it stand out a bit more:

```
<p class="black">Please register your visit using this
application.</p>
```

We have now applied the class 'black' to that paragraph. Now add the following code to the style section of your webpage:

```
.black{
    color:black;
}
```

Note: the . before 'black' tells the browser that we are looking for a class. A period, or full stop, is shorthand for class in CSS.

You should now find that the first paragraph is black, whilst the remaining paragraphs remain grey.

Classes allow us to provide specific CSS rules to as many elements as we like, and to elements of any type.

Note that the paragraph with class 'black' actually has two style rules applied to it. The p rule tells it to be grey, and the black rule tells it to be black. As CSS states that the most 'specific' rule should win out, rules defined by classes or IDs will always trump those applied to element types. So the paragraph ends up black, not grey. This is the 'cascading' part of Cascading Style Sheets in action.

IDs

IDs are very similar to classes, but they should only be applied to one element on a webpage. They are designed for elements that will only appear once, such as a header, footer or title.

We add them in exactly the same way as with classes, so try changing the opening h2 text to have an id of 'red':

```
<h2 id="red">Welcome to Coding Solutions
Enterprises&#8482;</h2>
```

Remove the h2 {color: red} rule from our CSS – after all, we may wish to use h2 tags elsewhere on our page and we don't want them all in our brand red. Now add the following CSS to the style section:

```
#red {
    color:red;
}
```

Note: *here we use a hash symbol, #, to represent an ID. So in CSS, . is short for class and # is short for ID.*

Remember rules relating to IDs and classes will always trump those related to element types.

PRACTICE EXERCISE

Add internal CSS to the webpage, available on exercise link CC10, to make the first paragraph red and the second paragraph blue using classes and IDs: [CC 12]

We can now select elements by either their type, or their class or ID. We have only learned one CSS rule though, which is how to change the colour of text. Before we look at other rules, we'll quickly see how we can use the <div>element to break up our code into different sections.

Divs

Div is short for 'division' and allows us to divide our code into different sections. This means we can style each section differently if we want to. Divs provide a useful container with which to contain and group together elements of a particular section of our page. They also provide and allow us to better structure our websites as we shall see. Add the following code to our webpage:

```
<div>
        <img src="http://completewebdevelopercourse.
com/star.png" width="100" height="100">
        <h2 id="red">Welcome to Coding Solutions
Enterprises&#8482;</h2>
        <p class="black">Please register your visit
using this application.</p>
    </div>

    <div>
        <p>Please read the following information:</p>
        <a href="#conduct">Code of Conduct</a>
    </div>

    <div>
        <p><strong>Important:</strong> Please have
the following information ready:</p>
        <ul>
            <li>License Plate</li>
            <li>Parking Bay Number</li>
            <li>Name Of Person You Are Visiting</li>
        </ul>
    </div>
```

The result should look like this (4.4):

4.4

Welcome to Coding Solutions Enterprises™

Please register your visit using this application.

Please read the following information:

Code of Conduct

Important: Please have the following information ready:

- License Plate
- Parking Bay Number
- Name Of Person You Are Visiting

```
 9            ol{color:gray;}
10            .black{color:black;}
11          </style>
12       </head>
13 >     <body>
14 >        <div>
15            <img src="http://completewebdevelopercourse.com/star.png" width="100" height="100">
16            <h2 id="red">Welcome to Coding Solutions Enterprises&#8482;</h2>
17            <p class="black">Please register your visit using this application.</p>
18          </div>
19
20 >        <div>
21            <p>Please read the following information:</p>
22            <a href="#conduct">Code of Conduct</a>
23          </div>
24
25 >        <div>
26            <p><strong>Important:</strong> Please have the following information ready:</p>
27 >           <ul>
28              <li>License Plate</li>
29              <li>Parking Bay Number</li>
30              <li>Name Of Person You Are Visiting</li>
31            </ul>
32          </div>
33
34          <input type="checkbox">Do you have a vehicle?
35          <input type="text">
36
```

The presentation hasn't changed! It might not look like the divs are doing very much, but they actually give us a lot of control over our design when we start applying styles to them. Let's start by giving them a background colour.

Background colours

We'll now look at a range of different CSS styles that we can use. We want to mark out the Information Requirements section. Add the following inline style to that div element like so:

```
<div style="background-color:aliceblue">
        <p><strong>Important:</strong> Please have
the following information ready:</p>
```

```
<ul>
    <li>License Plate</li>
    <li>Parking Bay Number</li>
    <li>Name Of Person You Are Visiting</li>
</ul>
</div>
```

This differentiates our requirements section a bit better (*4.5*):

4.5

Welcome to Coding Solutions Enterprises™

Please register your visit using this application.

Please read the following information:

Code of Conduct

Important: Please have the following information ready:

* License Plate
* Parking Bay Number
* Name Of Person You Are Visiting

```
 9        ol{color:gray}
10          .black{color:black}
11        </style>
12      </head>
13      <body>
14        <div>
15          <img src="http://completewebdeveloper.course.com/star.png" width="100" height="100">
16          <h2 id="red">Welcome to Coding Solutions Enterprises&#8482;</h2>
17          <p class="black">Please register your visit using this application.</p>
18        </div>
19
20        <div>
21          <p>Please read the following information:</p>
22          <a href="#conduct">Code of Conduct</a>
23        </div>
24
25        <div style="background-color:aliceblue">
26          <p><strong>Important:</strong> Please have the following information ready:</p>
27          <ul>
28            <li>License Plate</li>
29            <li>Parking Bay Number</li>
30            <li>Name Of Person You Are Visiting</li>
31          </ul>
32        </div>
33
34        <input type="checkbox">Do you have a vehicle?
35        <input type="text">
36
```

Note: The div stretches all the way across the browser window by default.

PRACTICE EXERCISE

Rather than using an inline style attribute, it would be better to define this background colour as a class. See if you can change the code to accomplish this.
Don't forget the . before the class name!

Colour codes

So far we've only used names to describe colours. As you can imagine, we usually want to be more precise than that, and we do that using colour codes, which are like HTML entities for colours, with each code representing a particular colour. Try these rules:

```
background-color: #765481;
background-color: #F7E1A2;
```

The hash symbol # tells the browser that we are going to use a number to represent the colour, and then we use a six-digit alphanumeric code (a code containing letters and numbers) for the colours that we want, in this case purple and orange.

You don't have to memorize all the codes – you can use a website like http://html-color-codes.info/ to work out the colour code for the colour that you want to use.

PRACTICE EXERCISE

Update the styling for the paragraphs to the appropriate colour, using HTML colour codes: **CC 13**

Changing sizes

We can use the *width* and *height* rules to change the width and height of our div. But first a little consolidation and restructuring. Add an id of 'intro' to our first div – this contains our branding and opening message. To make things simpler, let's remove our code of conduct link div and the elements within and also the code of conduct Latin text at the end of our page. Next add a class of 'infoBox' to the other div, ie the one with our information requirements. Place all our remaining elements below into another div with an id of 'questions'. Finally, add the following CSS styles:

```
#intro{
width:50%;
}
.infoBox{
background-color:aliceblue;
width:50%;
}
```

Your page and code should look like this (4.6):

4.6

Note that we can apply as many CSS rules to each element as we want. With CSS, we have to add units to our widths and heights, so 200px means '200 pixels' and '50%' means '50% of the containing element', in this case the <body> element.

Positioning with floats

So far we've seen how to use CSS to adjust colours and sizes, but we can also use CSS to affect layout. Up until now, all our elements have appeared below each other, but we can change that using *floats*. Try adding the following to the CSS rules:

```
#intro{
width:50%;
float:left;
}
  .infoBox{
background-color:aliceblue;
width:50%;
float:right;
}
#questions{
clear:both;
}
```

Your page should now look like this (4.7):

4.7

Notice what has happened: .infoBox is now 'floated' on the right of the page, and #intro is in line with it on the left. Try removing the CSS rule clear:both; from div #questions. You should see the questions start to display awkwardly, wrapping in the space around the other two divs as per the image below (4.8):

4.8

This is because the top two 'floated' divs cause the content of div #questions to 'flow' up into the space underneath the shorter. infoBox div on the right. This is an important gotcha when designing column layouts. The clear:both; rule that we previously had on div #questions ensured that the content of that div 'cleared' the other two floated divs above.

Make sure you put this CSS rule back in to make the presentation look right again:

```
#questions{
    clear:both;
}
```

Floats are an extremely useful way to arrange divs or other elements to the left or right of each other.

PRACTICE EXERCISE

Update the internal CSS on the webpage in exercise CC12 to make #left float left and #right float right: CC 14

Layout with positions

Sometimes we want to be even more precise with our layouts than floats can allow, and we do that with *positioning*. If we want to move the position of, say, div .infoBox, relative to where it would otherwise be, we can add the following CSS rules:

```
position: relative;
top: 50px;
```

This will move it 50 pixels down (4.9):

4.9

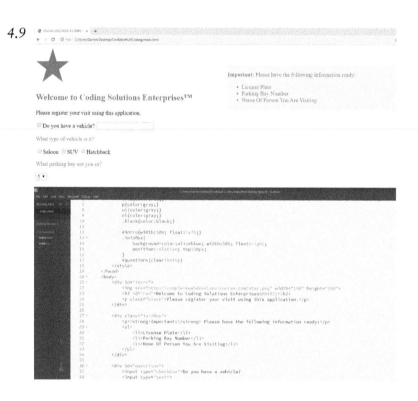

Try experimenting with different values of 'top' and 'left'.

Question: How do negative values (eg -50px) of 'top' and 'left' affect the position of the div?
Answer: They move it upwards and to the left.

So using position: relative will move the element relative to where it would otherwise be. Try adding:

```
position: absolute;
```

to the div .infoBox rules. What effect does that have? It actually removes the div from the flow of the page, so the other elements ignore its existence. This can be useful if you want to position an element relative to the page, rather than relative to other elements. You can still use 'top', 'left' and also 'bottom' and 'right' to move absolutely positioned objects around. Obviously, the overlap position currently is pretty useless (unless of course we wanted it to be a pop-up) – try positioning the .infoBox div over to the right of the page (*4.10*):

4.10

PRACTICE EXERCISE

Update the internal CSS to give the #home div an absolute position of 10 pixels right and 10 pixels down and the #next div a relative position of 50 pixels right and 10 pixels up: **CC 15**

Margins

Margins give an alternative, and in some ways simpler, way to position elements. To see it in action, remove all the positioning rules from div .infoBox and add the rule below to it instead:

```
margin: 20px;
```

This gives a 20-pixel margin around the .infoBox div, which looks like this (*4.11*):

4.11

But wait, what just happened to our layout? Well, if you think about it .infoBox is 50% of the page width and #intro, to its left, takes up the other 50%. We've then just added a margin of 20px all around .infoBox. This means all the space required by .infoBox is greater than what is available and so it is forced down below #intro in the flow of the page. We could just adjust the width of .infoBox so it takes up less space, but for now let's look at setting specific margins. We can set the top, bottom, left and right margins individually – delete the general margin rule, and let's add the following to .infoBox:

```
margin-top: 50px;
```

This effectively moves the blue div 50px down (*4.12*).

4.12

PRACTICE EXERCISE

Give the div with the ID box a margin of 10 pixels at the top, 15 pixels on either side and 20 pixels on the bottom setting each margin individually (eg margin-top) **CC 16**

Margins are a great way to move objects around and leave a gap where the object would have been. In a similar way, we can use padding to add a margin *inside* the element.

Padding

In all our divs, there is no padding around the text inside the div. Usually it's prettier to leave a gap between the text and the edge of the div, and we do that using padding. Try adding this rule to our divs using a CSS rule on the div element.

```
div
{

        padding:15px;

        box-sizing:border-box;

}
```

This adds 15 pixels of padding all around the inside of our divs (*4.13*):

4.13

You probably noticed that we snuck another CSS rule in there – box-sizing:border-box.

This style and value of 'border-box' ensures that any padding (and border for that matter) is included in the overall width and height of the element. In our case that's important because of our adjacent 50% width elements which would otherwise exceed the available space. Experiment by removing this rule – just remember to put it back in (*4.14*)!

4.14

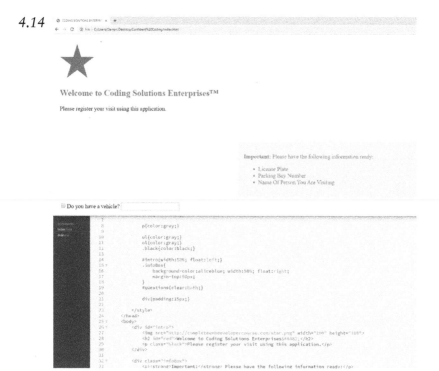

Try experimenting with padding-top, padding-bottom to see what effect they have.

Padding is a great way to add a little space within your elements, to give your content room to breathe.

PRACTICE EXERCISE

Style the #box div to have padding of 15px on the top, right, bottom and left sides with as few commands as you can: **CC 17**

Borders

Adding borders to your elements is a simple way to separate different parts of your webpage. Borders can make a complex page much more readable, and are a good way to bring in a little graphical flair without using images.

Let's add a border around our div .infoBox to demarcate it a bit more.

Add the following CSS:

```
border: solid 1px grey;
```

This will display as such (*4.15*):

4.15

Let's tone it down slightly (after all, we don't want it detracting from our logo and main instruction on the left):

```
border: dotted 0.5px grey;
```

This has the following effect (*4.16*):

Note that this style is a little different to the others we have seen so far, in that it includes three values:

- 1px: this is the width of the border.
- Solid: this is the border type. You can experiment with different border types, such as *dotted, dashed, groove* and *ridge.* You'll likely use solid most of the time though.

- Grey: this is the border colour. You can use any colour you like, or HTML colour codes such as #47D812.

Challenge 1

Create a top border on div #questions in order to show where our questions begin. Your code should look like this:

```
border-top: solid 1px #cccccc
```

And in action (*4.17*):

4.17

Borders can get pretty garish, so keep them simple.

Rounded corners

Related to borders are rounded corners. These were added in CSS 3, the latest version of the CSS language. To add them, we use the *border-radius* property. Try replacing the *border* style for div.info Box to:

```
border-radius: 5px;
```

4.18

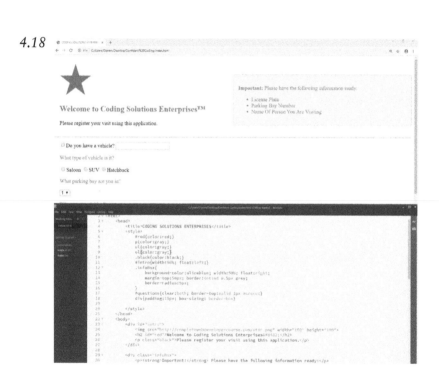

Now we have an attractive rounded rectangle (*4.18*). You can adjust the border-radius value to anything you like to increase the roundedness, but 5–10 pixels is usually about right for most situations.

Question: What happens when you set the border-radius to
50%? Why?
Answer: We get a circle.

We get a circle because the radius of the curved edge is equal to
half the width of the div (ie 100 pixels in this case). That means
there is no room left for any straight edges – the whole of the
border is rounded, and thus we are left with a circle.

Note that the rounded corner is only applied to the background and not the content – you would have to add some
padding to the div to position the text completely inside the
circle.

PRACTICE EXERCISE

Practise adding a simple border and rounded corners to two divs
here: **CC 18**

Fonts

Just like with a standard Word document, we can change the
fonts used on our Visitor Registration webpage. So far, we have
displayed all text in the browser's default font (in Chrome's case
this is a version of Times New Roman).

Add the following CSS style to the body element:

```
body{
    font-family: sans-serif;
}
```

Your page should now look like this (*4.19*):

4.19

This changes the text to the browser's default sans serif font.

Sans serif means without serifs, ie without decorative lines or 'ticks' at the end of each letter. Sans serif fonts are usually seen as more modern and cleaner than serif fonts.

Note: we have applied the font-family property to the body, not the paragraph element. This means that all text on the page will be affected, which is usually what we want, as most webpages use just one font.

Fancier fonts

We don't have to limit our application to the default serif and sans serif fonts, we can use any font we like. However, if our website is popular, it will be accessed from a range of different devices, which may not have the font that we want to use installed. In this case, we can set up a list of fonts, and the webpage will use the first one that is available.

A nice example of this is the 'Better Helvetica' CSS trick at https://css-tricks.com/snippets/css/better-helvetica/

```
body {
    font-family: "HelveticaNeue-Light", "Helvetica
Neue Light", "Helvetica Neue", Helvetica, Arial, "Lucida
Grande", sans-serif;
}
```

Helvetica Neue is a font known for being modern, simple and stylish, but only Apple devices make it available as a default. Change our body CSS to the above. This CSS style will select that font if it is available, but offers a range of fallbacks to pick the 'prettiest' version of the font available as you can see on the right (4.20):

4.20

It is generally recommended to stick to 'web safe fonts' if you want to be confident that all your users will see the font that you intend. To get a list of these fonts, just type 'web safe fonts' into your favourite search engine.

PRACTICE EXERCISE

Create some text using the Georgia web safe font with a fallback of serif: CC 19

Styling text

We can do a lot more with text than just set the font – we can make text bold, italic, underlined, and a lot more. Currently our webpage company name looks a little dated – perhaps trying too hard to be noticed – let's give it a more contemporary feel by adding the following to the #red CSS rule:

```
#red{

        color:red;
        font-weight:lighter;

}
```

See this in action (*4.21*):

4.21

But we should differentiate the text 'Welcome to' from our company name. To do that, we'll need to introduce a new element called *span*. In itself, this element does nothing, but it allows us to style individual parts of an element. Try replacing the paragraph HTML with:

```
<h2 id="red"><span id="standout">Welcome to</span>
Coding Solutions Enterprises&#8482;</h2>
```

The span element in itself doesn't affect the style of the text at all (*4.22*):

4.22

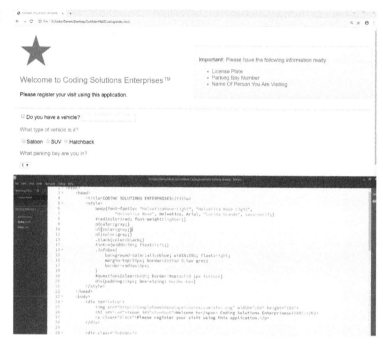

However, it does allow us to apply a style only to the contents of the span:

```
#standout{
        font-weight:bold;
}
```

Remember #standout is just a CSS id and simply means 'apply these CSS rules to the element with an ID of standout'.

Now only the words 'Welcome to' are in bold (4.23):

4.23

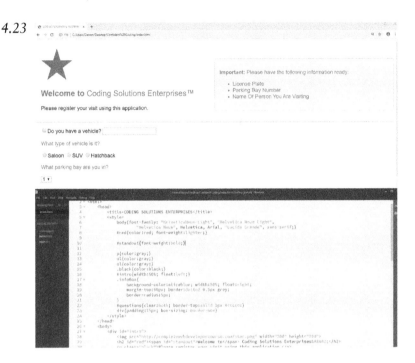

Similarly, we can use a second style on this span to add some italicized text.

Change the CSS rule to read:

```
#standout{font-weight:bold; font-style:italic}
```

Your code output should look like this (4.24):

4.24

Challenge 2

The CSS rule to underline text is *text-decoration: underline*. Have a go at underlining the word 'Important' in the div .infoBox.

Your HTML should look like this:

```
<p><strong class="underlined">Important:</strong>
Please have the following information ready:</p>
```

And your CSS should have this rule:

```
.underlined{
        text-decoration: underline;
}
```

The final outcome should look like this (*4.25*):

4.25

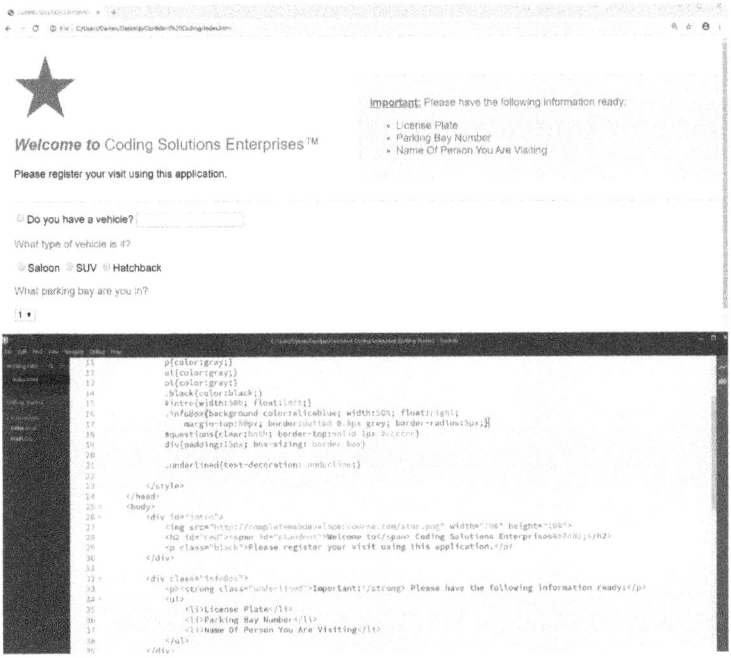

You can of course combine these styles to have bold and underlined text, and there are other text styling options – you can see more of them at www.w3schools.com/css/css_text.asp

---

PRACTICE EXERCISE

Use CSS to make some text bold and italic: **CC 20**

Aligning text

Just like in a word processor, you can use CSS to align text left, right or justified (so that the words spread out to fill the space available). To align the text to the right, just add the following style:

```
text-align: right;
```

To set the text to be aligned to the left, use:

```
text-align: left;
```

This is the default, so you don't usually need to use it. For justified, just use:

```
text-align: justify;
```

Note that you'll need to have enough text to go over the end of the line to see this in action.

This works well with long pieces of text such as blog articles, but not so well with general website content, so use sparingly.

PRACTICE EXERCISE

Practise setting text to be justified here: **CC 21**

Styling links

Links can be styled like any other HTML element, but there are a couple of settings that you'll likely want to use specifically with links.

The first is to remove the underlining of links – this has become unfashionable in recent years, with links usually being identified using colour. To remove the underline from a link, just use the style:

```
text-decoration: none;
```

More interestingly, we can also use what are known as *pseudo classes* to style what a link looks like when it is hovered over by the user. To do this, use:

```
a:hover {
    color: green;
}
```

Combining these two commands gives us a link that is not underlined, and turns green when you hover over it.

A pseudo class is so named because is not a 'real' class in that it doesn't refer directly to an element, but to a particular state of that element, in this case the hover state. So it's not a normal class that we define, but a particular 'state', such as when a link is hovered over, or if the element is the first one in a list. If you want to learn more about pseudo classes you can do so at www.w3schools.com/css/css_pseudo_classes.asp.

Open in a new tab

This is not strictly a CSS command, but while we are styling links, having the option to open a link in a new tab or browser window can be very handy. We can do this by adding target= _"blank" to the link, like this:

```
<a href="http://www.google.com" target=_"blank">Click me
to open Google.com in a new tab.</a>
```

PRACTICE EXERCISE

Practise styling links and opening them in new tabs: CC 22

CSS project: clone a website

A great way to practise CSS is to clone a website that you like the look of. You could start with something fairly simple, like www.google.com, and move on to something a little more complicated, such as www.bbc.co.uk/news. Pick any site you like, and try to create an accurate copy of it. It's not an easy task (and it will probably involve plenty of googling), but you'll learn a huge amount in the process.

When you're done, paste your code into a site like codepen.com, and share the link with Rob on Twitter (@techedrob). We look forward to seeing what you can create.

Summary

Congratulations, you now know the basics of CSS. You know how to add a range of styles, layouts and formatting to a website, and combined with the HTML skills you learned in the previous chapter, you should be able to design pretty much any website you like.

Having covered HTML (for content) and CSS (for style and layout), we will now be moving on to learning JavaScript, for interactivity. JavaScript will allow you to add a huge amount of power to your webpages, allowing the user to interact with them just like they would an app or piece of software.

JavaScript is a whole new world of coding, so let's get started.

Further learning

As before, we would advise moving on to JavaScript for now, but if you've got the CSS bug, these further learning links will help you learn more about cascading style sheets.

- www.codecademy.com/courses/css-coding-with-style/0/1 (archived at https://perma.cc/UU6Z-Q7XR) – interactive CSS coding lessons.
- www.w3schools.com/css/ (archived at https://perma.cc/3Q28-YJZL) – CSS tutorials from W3Schools.
- http://learnlayout.com (archived at https://perma.cc/FEC5-V3PR) – create great flexible layouts with CSS.
- https://play.google.com/store/apps/details?id=com.sololearn. csstrial&hl=en (archived at https://perma.cc/S4JK-S7EK)– Android app to teach you CSS.
- https://itunes.apple.com/gb/app/learn-css/id953955717? mt=8 (archived at https://perma.cc/47V3-999Q) – iPhone and iPad app to teach you CSS.

## CHAPTER FIVE

JavaScript

We've now made use of HTML for content, and CSS for style and layout for our Visitor Registration page. It's time to bring in the third piece of the puzzle, JavaScript, which allows for interaction with the user. Unlike HTML and CSS, JavaScript is a 'full' programming language in the sense that we can use it to run computer programs: pieces of software that can do pretty much anything the coder wants.

In this chapter, we'll cover:

- what JavaScript is and how it is used;
- how we can make use of JavaScript on our page to add interactivity;
- running JavaScript in response to a user action such as a click; and
- how to use JavaScript to:
  - change the content and style of webpages;
  - use programming fundamentals such as loops and if statements;
  - generate random numbers.

What is JavaScript?

JavaScript is our first 'proper' coding language. It allows us to use programming tools such as loops, variables and if statements (we'll find out what these are shortly). It can be used for a whole range of tasks, from making a piece of text disappear when we click on it to creating full apps, such as the Google Docs suite of office applications.

Any website that provides interactivity without reloading the page uses JavaScript.

JavaScript was created in 10 days in May 1995 by Brendan Eich, working at Netscape, one of the first browsers. It was originally called Mocha, and then Livescript. Interestingly, it has nothing to do with the Java programming language beyond the name. Netscape was given permission from Sun (who owned the Java language) to use the name JavaScript, primarily as a marketing technique, as Java was a very popular language at the time.

JavaScript has gone through many iterations and developments, but the latest standard version (which we will learn here) is supported in all browsers, on both desktop and mobile platforms.

One important aspect of JavaScript is that it runs on the user's computer, rather than a server. This makes it what is known as a *client-side language*. Therefore to do anything requiring a server,

5.1

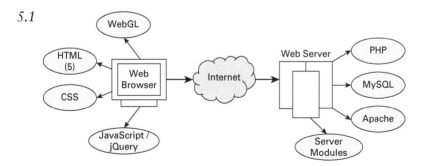

such as send an email, or signing up a user to your new social network, you'll need to use a *server-side language* such as Python, which we will learn in the next chapter.

Why learn JavaScript?

If you're not convinced already, the benefits of learning JavaScript are many. Primarily, it is our first 'proper' programming language, allowing us to develop full, interactive apps and websites, rather than just create layouts and static webpages.

It's also very similar to a number of other languages, so once you learn JavaScript, you'll be able to get started with any other language much more quickly.

As JavaScript works in all browsers, you don't need to download any extra software to get started with it. And it uses classes and IDs, just like CSS, so it's strongly linked to what you have already learned.

It's a simple language to get started with, but as with CSS is hugely powerful, and so is a great first coding language to learn.

What does JavaScript look like?

JavaScript is very simple to get started with. To begin, let's return to our Visitor Registration application, specifically the last line in our code:

```
<input type="submit" value="Confirm">
```

It should look like this (5.2):

5.2

Ideally, when we click on this button we would like the page to acknowledge submission of our visit details. Of course, when you click the button at the moment, nothing happens. Let's change that with some JavaScript magic. Change the button code to the following:

```
<input onclick='alert("Guest Registered")' type=
"submit" value="Confirm">
```

(Make sure you get the right type of quotation marks – we need ' on the outside and " on the inside.)

When you click the button, you should now see this (5.3):

5.3

Hurrah, you've run your first piece of JavaScript! The *onclick* attribute allows us to write some JavaScript which will be run when the button is clicked. The actual JavaScript we are running is:

```
alert("Guest Registered")
```

The *alert* command means 'create a popup window with a message for the user', and that message is contained within the single quote marks, ie Guest Registered. In JavaScript a command is usually followed by parentheses, or brackets, containing information for the command. In this case, the information is the text to be displayed in the popup.

PRACTICE EXERCISE

Change the code so that instead of alerting Guest Registered it alerts a friendlier confirmation message.

Your code should look something like this:

```
<input onclick='alert("Welcome, your visit has been
registered.")' type="submit" value="Confirm">
```

Running JavaScript like this is known as *inline JavaScript*, just like *inline CSS* as we saw at the beginning of the previous chapter.

Internal JavaScript

Running JavaScript like this is much like running CSS using the *style* attribute – it works, but it's messy, and is a frustrating experience if you are trying to write more than a simple alert command.

Just like CSS, we can separate out our JavaScript from our HTML using *internal JavaScript*. With CSS we used <style>tags, and with JavaScript we use <script>tags. Those tags can go in the header of our HTML page, but we'll be putting them at the end of the page. This is generally good practice, as it makes sure all the elements of the page have been created by the browser before we try and run JavaScript on them.

To create some JavaScript which alerts *Welcome, please register your visit.* when the page is loaded, add this code to your HTML page, just before the </body> tag:

```
<script>
    alert("Welcome, please register your visit.")
</script>
```

You'll now see the alert popup when the page is loaded (you might need to refresh the page to see this effect), like this (5.4):

5.4

Internal JavaScript – responding to a click

When we used inline JavaScript, it was obvious which element was going to trigger the JavaScript, because the onclick attribute was within that element. So how do we associate our internal JavaScript with the button? The answer is the same as with CSS – we use IDs.

Challenge 1

Remove the onclick attribute from the button, and give it an ID of 'confirmation-button'.

Your button code should now look like this:

```
<input id="confirmation-button" type="submit"
value="Confirm">
```

Now, to make something happen when that button is clicked. First remove the alert code between the script tags that we used to display a message when the page loads. Then put the following code between the <script>tags in its place:

```
document.getElementById("confirmation-button").
onclick = function() {
    alert("Welcome, your visit has been registered.")
    }
```

This is perhaps the most complex code we have seen so far, but it's fairly straightforward when you break it down.

First, 'document' refers to the HTML page itself, telling the browser that we will be looking for something within the page.

Next getElementById("confirmation-button") does exactly what it says – it gets an element by its ID, in this case the ID is 'confirmation-button'.

The 'onclick = function()' part means we are setting the onclick attribute of our element equal to a function (a function is just a chunk of code that does something). The empty parentheses just mean that we are not passing any values to that function.

The { and }, known as curly brackets, contain the code for the function. Curly brackets are the standard way in JavaScript and many other languages to contain code for functions.

Finally, within the curly brackets we have our familiar alert ('Welcome, your visit has been registered.') which displays the alert.

All together in plain English, the code means:

Take the HTML page and find within it an element with an ID of 'confirmation-button'.
Then alter that element so that when the user clicks on it, it will display an alert with a text of 'Welcome, your visit has been registered.' Simple!

You may want to re-read the above paragraphs a couple of times to get everything clear, and then try this challenge.

Challenge 2

Display a further information pop-up if the user clicks on our star logo. Locate the image tag at the top of the page which displays our star logo. Now give it a ID of 'logo'. Now see if you can put in some code like we did with the button to respond to a click event.

Your code should look like this:

```
document.getElementById("logo").onclick = function() {
    alert("Coding Solutions Enterprises is an
organisation psuhing the boundaries of technological
innovation. We drive change through technical
enhancement in the workplace.")
    }
```

And in action (5.5):

5.5

PRACTICE EXERCISE

Add JavaScript to popup Button Clicked! when the button is clicked on the page: **CC 23**

Changing styles with JavaScript

As well as displaying alerts, we can change styles with JavaScript as well.

Challenge 3

Up until now, we have just assumed that the user has entered all the required information before clicking on submit. We'll come onto validation of the user entries in the following section, but for now let's display a simple validation message to the user immediately below the submit button.

Add a div with a paragraph of text immediately below the button. Give these elements IDs of validation-box and validation-message respectively:

```
<div id='validation-box'>
<p id='validation-message'>Please ensure all information
is entered correctly.</p>
</div>
```

Let's add some styles in the CSS (while we're at it, let's create some space around our submit button, too):

```
#confirmation-button{margin-top:25px; margin-
bottom:15px;}
#validation-box{border:solid 1px gray; display:none}
#validation-message{font-style:italic; margin:0;}
```

Important – did you notice that we set the display property of the validation box to 'none'? This is because we want it to be hidden until the user clicks on submit.

Now, change the code for the confirmation button to:

```
document.getElementById("confirmation-button").onclick =
function() {
        document.getElementById("validation-message").
        style.color = "red";
        document.getElementById("validation-box").style.
        display = "block";
}
```

The result should be that when the user clicks on the submit button, our validation message displays below, and the message text is red.

5.6

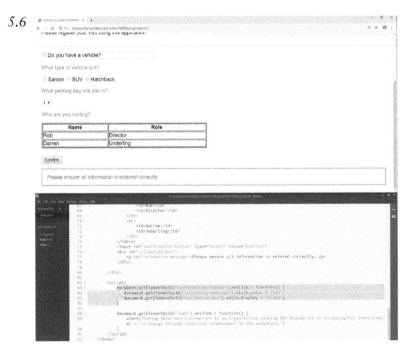

Tip: Whenever you are writing some new JavaScript, it can be a good idea to set up a separate simple page to make sure everything is 'wired up' and working correctly. Otherwise you can spend a lot of time debugging your code before realizing you forgot to capitalize the 'I' in getElementById!

Now let's add some detail to the validation message. Firstly, add in an input for the user's name and put it as the first item above vehicle registration. Give this an ID of input-name. Let's also take the opportunity to put div tags around each of our questions. This will make sure that they display on separate lines and keep things tidy:

```html
<div id="questions">
    <div>
        <p>Please enter your name</p>
        <input id="input-name" type="text">
    </div>

    <div>
        <input type="checkbox">Do you have a vehicle?
        <input type="text">
    </div>
    <div>
        <p>What type of vehicle is it?</p>
        <input type="radio" name="size">Saloon
        <input type="radio" name="size">SUV
        <input type="radio" name="size">Hatchback
    </div>
    <div>
        <p>What parking bay are you in?</p>
        <select>
            <option>1</option>
            <option>2</option>
            <option>3</option>
```

```
    </select>
</div>
<div>
    <p>Who are you visiting?</p>
    <table border="1">
    <tr>
        <th width="200">Name</th>
        <th width="300">Role</th>
    </tr>
    <tr>
        <td>Rob</td>
        <td>Director</td>
    </tr>
    <tr>
        <td>Darren</td>
        <td>Underling</td>
    </tr>
    </table>
</div>

<input id="confirmation-button" type="submit"
  value="Confirm">
<div id="validation-box">
    <p id="validation-message">Please ensure all
    information is entered correctly.</p>
</div>
</div>
```

Next add another line of code for the submit (confirmation-button):

```
document.getElementById("validation-message").innerHTML =
    "Please ensure all fields are completed.";
```

Give it a go! You should see when you click submit that your JavaScript code sets the paragraph text. We make use of the innerHTML property here to set the HTML contained within the paragraph tag – in this case, just simple text.

Now let's personalize the message a bit more. Change that line of code to the following:

```
document.getElementById("validation-message").innerHTML
    = document.getElementById("input-name").value + ",
    please ensure all fields are completed.";
```

5.7

Now we are getting some real interaction, so it's time to learn a couple of fundamental programming concepts. The first is an 'if statement'.

If statements

If statements are absolutely fundamental to programming. They instruct the program to do something only if a condition is met. This might be logging into your favourite website – 'if the user-name and password match an entry in the database, log the user in'. Or it might be one of the rules in a game – 'if Mario touches the bomb, kill Mario'.

5.8

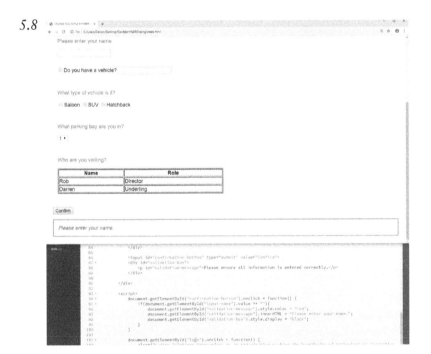

In our application, we have pulled the user's name into the validation message to give some personalization. But what if the user name is not set? And what about the other fields that might be required – such as the vehicle registration number?

Let's change our code to make the validation in our application a bit more meaningful and useful. Replace the code for the confirmation-button click with the following:

```
if(document.getElementById("input-name").value == ""){
    document.getElementById("validation-message").style.
color = "red";
    document.getElementById("validation-message").
innerHTML = "Please enter your name.";
    document.getElementById("validation-box").style.
display = "block";
}
```

If you look carefully at the code, you should be able to see what is going on. We start with the 'if' keyword, and then we have our condition in parentheses. The condition here is that the value in the text box must be equal to blank text, ie nothing has been entered. If that is the case the system will display our validation message and prompt the user to enter their name. If not, it will do nothing (note, you will need to refresh the page to reset the input box and hide the validation message between attempts).

Notice the double equals == here. In JavaScript (and almost all programming languages), we use a single equals to *set* something equal to something else, like when we set the onclick attribute equal to the function in the screenshot above. We use a *double equals* to test if something is equal to something else. It's a distinction you'll need to get used to, and your code will behave very strangely if (when!) you get it the wrong way round.

You can also use != instead of ==. This, as you have probably guessed, checks to see if something is /not/ equal. Try it out! If you change our code from == to !=, you should see the behaviours reversed: when something is entered, our message is displayed, and when it is blank, nothing happens. This is obviously incorrect – so make sure to change it back when you're done testing (5.9)!

5.9

After you have set the if condition back to ==, consider that the user *has* entered a name. We now have the information required; the if == " " is false ,and so we don't need to execute the code that displays the validation message. But it would be useful to execute some other code at this point, and we can do that using the *else* keyword. Add the following just after the final } in the if statement:

```
if(document.getElementById("input-name").value != ""){
        document.getElementById("validation-
message").style.color = "red";
        document.getElementById("validation-
message").innerHTML = "Please enter your name.";
        document.getElementById("validation-box").
style.display = "block";
    }else{
        alert(document.getElementById
("input-name").value + ", your registration has been
submitted.");
        }
```

Now if we have entered a name we will receive the familiar confirmation message (*5.10*):

5.10

Challenge 4

So far, we have accounted for just the one validation on the user's name. Moving our attention to the other input elements, let's see how we can validate them too. Let's assume for now that the user has driven to our premises. Provided the user has entered a name, can you change the code to also check to see that a license plate has been provided? Remember to add the ID to the license plate input. Your code should look something like this:

```
document.getElementById("confirmation-button").onclick =
function() {
    if(document.getElementById("input-name").value == ""){
    document.getElementById("validation-message").
    style.color = "red";
        document.getElementById("validation-message").
        innerHTML = "Please enter your name.";
        document.getElementById("validation-box").style.
        display = "block";
    }else{
    if(document.getElementById("input-license").value ==
""){ document.getElementById("validation-message").
style.color = "red";
        document.getElementById("validation-message").
innerHTML = "Please enter a vehicle license.";
        document.getElementById("validation-box").style.
display = "block";
    }else{
```

```
        alert (document.getElementById("input-name").
value + ", your registration has been submitted.");
                    }

                }

            }
```

This is an example of nesting if else statements. Take a moment to follow through the code and the different conditions and results. Using nesting in this way, we can add in additional control to the logic and flow of our code.

And in action (*5.11*):

5.11

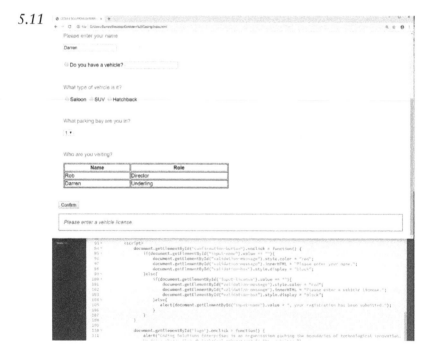

PRACTICE EXERCISE

Update the value of x so the if statement gives the output x is less than five: (**CC 24**)

Updating website content

Before we learn the second fundamental programming concept (loops), let's return to updating our website content with JavaScript. We've used an alert to display the success message to the user. Whilst alerts are useful, they can be rather distracting, and we also have limited control over their behaviours and appearance.

Challenge 5

Remove the alert code that displays our success message and, in its place, let's insert the following code:

```
}else{;
    document.getElementById("validation-message").
innerHTML = "Your registration has been submitted.";
    document.getElementById("validation-box").style.
display = "block";
}
```

And in action (*5.12*):

5.12

We have now removed the alert and instead we make use of the validation box to display our success message, just like we did for our validation errors. One thing you may have noticed is that we now have some unnecessary duplication of code in our submit click event. Because we are now displaying the validation box for both validation errors and success messages, we are always going to set the display style to block. We can therefore place a single statement of:

```
document.getElementById("validation-box").style.display
= "block";
```

before the If statement and remove the other duplicate instances. Regularly inspecting your code and making it more efficient is a necessary step as your applications grow in scope and capabilities. Your code should now look like *5.13* below, and the output should be the same as before.

5.13

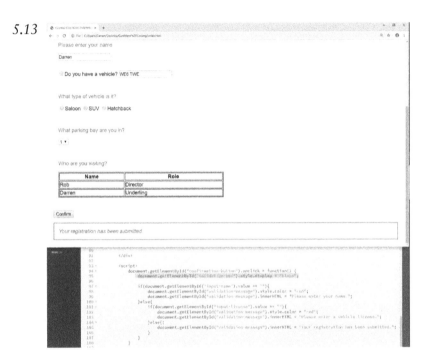

Challenge 6

So, we have a success message displayed, but really it could do with a bit more prominence.

Let's add some dynamic styling in the event of a successful submission. Add the following CSS class to the style rules:

```
.success-box{
    background-color:#addcb6;
    position:fixed;
    width:300px;
    top:50%; left:50%;
    translate:transform(-50%,-50%);
}
```

The position property causes the be displayed in a fixed spot on the page and by setting top and left to 50% we place the box directly in the centre. However, the element is positioned based on the top left corner. Now obviously because the element has a width set above to 300px and an inherent height our box would be slightly off-centre. To remedy this, we introduce the translate:transform(-50%,-50%); rule – this essentially says shift our box to the left and up by 50% of its width and height, therefore ensuring a perfect centre placement on our screen.

We won't see our styles just yet because we haven't assigned our class to the validation box element yet. Now normally we would simply add class="success-box" to our element. However, in this instance we need the class to be applied dynamically, that is only when we are showing the success message and the validation is satisfied. We can do this with the following code:

```
document.getElementById("validation-box").classList.
add("success-box");
```

This line of code dynamically adds the class 'success-box' to our validation-box element. The style rules of the class 'success-box' are then applied. You should see the following results (5.14):

5.14

Loops

Loops are a way of repeating the same action again and again. Twitter uses loops to display a timeline of tweets, and Google uses them to display your search results. It's fair to say software as we know it wouldn't exist without loops.

We are going to leave our Visitor Registration webpage at this stage to focus more on coding and functionality concepts in the coming section and chapters. But don't worry, we'll continue to explore programming within the context of our Visitor Registration project so that we have a natural point of reference.

Make sure you save your work using the File > Save As menu command. Then select Close All from the File menu. You should now be left with the Getting Started template files. Select File > Live Preview and this will automatically create a new instance for us – you should see the Getting Started page and code again. Clear out all of the Getting Started content and put in some script tags and a div with an ID = "numbers" leaving the following structure:

```
<!DOCTYPE html>
<html>
    <head>
        <meta charset="utf-8">
        <meta http-equiv="X-UA-Compatible"
content="IE=edge">
        <title>Programming Loops</title>
    </head>
    <body>
        <div id="numbers"></div>
        <script>

        </script>
    </body>
</html>
```

A nice feature of our application might be the ability to print out all the available car parking bays. To get started we're going to create a simple loop to display the numbers 1 to 50 on our page. To do this we will need a *variable* to keep track of the number that we are on as we go through the loop. A variable is just a container for a number or some text, and we create one with the keyword *var*.

```
var number = 1
```

This creates a variable called 'number' and sets its value to 1. The loop then works like this:

```
while (number <= 50) {
        document.getElementById("numbers").innerHTML +=
        "<p>" + number + "</p>"
            number = number + 1
}
```

The 'while' keyword here means 'keep doing this code as long as this condition is true'. The condition is that the variable *number* has to be less than or equal to 50. Then, within the curly brackets ('the loop'), we add the current number, wrapped in <p>tags, to the content of the numbers div (that's what the += does). Finally, we add 1 to *number*, and repeat the loop until *number* is bigger than 50.

You might want to read that through a couple of times, and of course try it out for yourself. When you do you should see this (*5.15*):

5.15

The list on the left goes all the way down to 50.

PRACTICE EXERCISES

Now suppose our car parking roster is slightly more complicated. Change the above code so that it displays:

1   Only even numbered bays are available for visitors. Display all the even numbers up to 100.

2   Changing the parking allocation again: only spaces 0 through 10 are now available to visitors. Due to the parking lot layout the higher bay numbers are closer to the entrance, therefore display these new visitor bay numbers in descending order.

Answers:

1 Just change the first line in the loop to:
   var number = 2
       and the while statement to:
   while (number <= 100)
       and the last line to:
   number = number + 2
       That will generate all the even numbers from 2 to 100.

2 For this challenge, change the first line to:
   var number = 10
       and the while statement to:
   while (number >= 0)
       and the last line to:
   number = number – 1
       You then have a countdown from 10 to 0.

For loops

There is a second type of loop that you should be aware of. So far we have focused on *while* loops, but there are also *for* loops, which do the same thing but are structured slightly differently. A for loop looks like this:

```
for (var i = 1; i <= 50; i=i+1) {
    document.getElementById("numbers").innerHTML +=
"<p>" + i + "</p>"
    }
```

Unlike a while loop, in a for loop all the information about the for loop is contained in a single line. In this case the counter variable is called i (a commonly used letter in for loops), and it starts at 1, increases by 1 each time and continues until i is no longer equal to or less than 50. The effect is exactly the same as with while loops – which you use depends on context and personal preference. For what it's worth, we generally prefer while loops as we find they are more flexible.

Generating random numbers

It would be useful to have a feature that allowed us to allocate a random parking bay number to the visitor (for the purposes of our current example we will assume the bays are all available). We can achieve this using an inbuilt JavaScript function:

```
Math.random()
```

Remove the current code. Try adding this code:

```
document.getElementById("numbers").innerHTML = Math.random()
```

You'll see it generates a random decimal number between 0 and 1 (5.16):

5.16

For the purposes of our parking bays example we need a random whole number between 1 and 10. To do that we use this function:

```
Math.floor((Math.random() * 10)) + 1
```

This isn't as impenetrable as it looks! The '* 10' means 'multiply by 10' so we now have a random number between 0 and 10. The Math.floor part 'floors' the number by removing everything after the decimal point (so 6.74628748 would become 6). This gives us a random number between 0 and 9, so we add 1 to it to get a number between 1 and 10.

Try it out by changing your code in the above page to:

```
document.getElementById("numbers").innerHTML = Math.
floor((Math.random() * 10)) + 1
```

PRACTICE EXERCISE

Generate a random whole number between:

1   1 and 5

2   11 and 20

3   0 and 100

Answers:

1   Math.floor((Math.random() * 5)) + 1

2   Math.floor((Math.random() * 10)) + 10

3   Math.floor((Math.random() * 100))

JavaScript project: guessing game

Using variable, loops and if statements, you have the power to make a whole range of apps, websites and games. Let's have a little break from all this serious line-of-business application coding and have a look at something a bit more light-hearted. We're going to be working on a simple guessing game, where you have to guess the number that the computer has chosen.

The concept is pretty simple – when we load the page, the user will be asked to guess a random number between 1 and 10. If they get it wrong, they will be told whether they were too high or too low. If they get it right, they will be told so and given the chance to play again.

This challenge will involve putting together almost everything we've learned so far – interacting with elements, changing styles, variables and if statements. You are welcome to stop reading now and attempt the challenge, but we would advise working it through in stages, which we will do using mini-challenges.

The process would be similar to designing any website or app – start with the user interface, and then add the interactions gradually, checking that everything is working as you go.

Part 1: Create the user interface (a title (use an h1 element), instructions, a text input and a submit button)

There are many possible layouts, but mine is fairly simple (*5.17*):

```
<h1>What's My Number?</h1>
<p>I'm thinking of a number between 1 and 10 - what do
    you think it is?</p>
<input type="text">
<button>Guess</button>
```

5.17

Part 2: Basic interactivity (display the number that the user has entered)

Add in IDs for the elements and an empty paragraph, and fill it with the user's guess when they press the button (*5.18*):

5.18

```
<h1>What's My Number?</h1>
<p>I'm thinking of a number between 1 and 10 - what do
   you think it is?</p>
<input type="text" id="number">
<button id="guess">Guess</button>
```

```
<p id="message"></p>
<script>
          document.getElementById("guess").onclick =
          function() {
          document.getElementById("message").
          innerHTML =
          document.getElementById("number").value
          }
          </script>
```

Part 3: Add in the random number generator and check the user's guess against that number, displaying an appropriate message

We don't need to change the HTML at all now – it's all in the JavaScript:

```
if (document.getElementById("number").value >
      randomNumber) {
      document.getElementById("message").innerHTML =
      "Too High!"
      } else if (document.getElementById("number").
      value < randomNumber) {
      document.getElementById("message").innerHTML =
      "Too Low!"
      } else {
      document.getElementById("message").innerHTML =
      "That's it!"
      }
```

We have one slightly new construction here: *else if*. This allows you to test another if statement if the first one turns out to be false. Then we have a final *else* at the end, which will be processed if the first two statements are false. If the guess is not higher or lower than the number, it must be the right answer!

Try it out (*5.19*):

5.19

Part 4: Change the colour of the text depending on whether the answer is correct (green for yes, red for no) and give the option to play again

We use the following to change the text colour:

```
document.getElementById("text").style.color = "red"
```

To 'play again' we can just reload the page. We can do that with an empty link (<a href="">) so let's add that to the success message.

Here we go (5.20):

5.20

That's it. You've made a fully functional, interactive game using HTML, CSS and JavaScript – congratulations!

Summary

This is of course just the beginning of what JavaScript is capable of, and if you want to experiment further there are a lot of options. Try thinking of simple games that you could recreate in

JavaScript, such as simulating a coin toss, hangman, or even something like Snake from the old Nokia phones. There are numerous tutorials and guides online – just Google what you want to do followed by the words 'JavaScript tutorial' and you'll probably find something relevant!

Now that we've covered HTML for website content, CSS for style and layout, and JavaScript for interaction, we'll be looking at our first server-side language, Python.

Python is a simple and clean language, and similar to JavaScript in many ways. We'll see how we can build more complex structures with it, and make more sophisticated programs.

There's a lot to learn, and a lot of fun to be had too. Without further ado, let's jump in and see what we can achieve with Python.

Further learning

If you want to dip your toe a little deeper into the world of JavaScript, you can use these links to experiment further and learn more:

- www.codecademy.com/learn/javascript (archived at https://perma.cc/59R4-N9CN) – interactive JavaScript lessons.
- www.w3schools.com/JS/ (archived at https://perma.cc/T6KA-WUL2) – free JavaScript tutorials.
- www.learn-js.org (archived at https://perma.cc/ML5X-Y4UN) – free interactive JavaScript tutorials.
- https://play.google.com/store/apps/details?id=com.sololearn.javascript&hl=en_GB (archived at https://perma.cc/8SDX-3426) – learn JavaScript on Android.
- https://itunes.apple.com/gb/app/learn-javascript/id952738987?mt=8 (archived at https://perma.cc/8CEG-4XT3) – learn JavaScript on iPhone or iPad.

## CHAPTER SIX

Python

At the risk of boring you silly, let's quickly recap what we've learned so far. We started off looking at HTML, which allowed us to add content to webpages. Then we learned CSS, which we could use alongside the HTML to add styles and customize the layout of our webpage. Next, we saw how we could use JavaScript, our first 'proper' programming language, to make our pages interactive and allow the user to do something on our page and get a response.

So what's missing in our coding armoury? Well, so far everything we are doing happens completely in the user's browser. To be able to build software that allows users to communicate with each other, we need something called a *server*. A server is essentially a computer that is always on and always connected to the internet. Our computer can then contact that server to download information, save some content on the server (such as our latest tweet) or send data (such as an email) to another computer.

6.1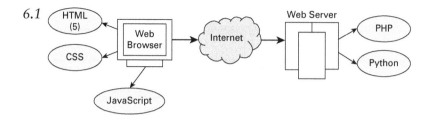

Therefore to be able to build truly powerful websites and apps, we need to write code that can run on a server. Although it is possible to use JavaScript on a server, it is more common to use other languages such as PHP or Python.

Here we are going to use Python, for several reasons:

- Python is a simple and straightforward language, even more so than JavaScript;
- Python can be used to build software on almost any platform, from servers to a Raspberry Pi, enabling you to build anything from websites to robots; and
- Python can be used to automate daily tasks, such as getting information from websites or automatically renaming your files (we'll see how to do that later in this chapter).

What is Python?

Python was developed in the late 1980s by Guido Van Rossum in the Netherlands. Van Rossum named the language after Monty Python, being a big fan of their Flying Circus.

Van Rossum is still actively involved in the development of the language, and as such has been given the title Benevolent Dictator For Life (BDFL) by the Python community.

Since its birth it has gone through a number of versions, and is currently at version 3. It is used widely to build both web-based and desktop applications, as well as on Internet Of Things devices such as the Arduino. This makes it an extremely powerful and flexible language to learn.

Why learn Python?

I don't want to build robots, do I really need to learn another language?

If you are not looking for a career in coding, you might be wondering if it's worth learning a second language after JavaScript. The answer is, of course, yes, but why?

Learning two languages allows you to see what languages have in common (and what they don't). Once you know how to create a loop in two languages, you'll be much clearer on what the critical parts of a loop are. The same is true with if statements and variables. Every language has its own idiosyncrasies, and if you only learn one language you won't have much insight into what they are.

So stick with me – even if you're not convinced that learning two languages is useful, if you ever have to extract, for example, all the email addresses from a webpage, Python can do that for you (and we'll see how at the end of the chapter).

What will this chapter cover?

As usual, we'll go through the whole process of running some Python, building up our skills and then practising with a few projects and exercises.

We'll also be working towards a larger side project to our Visitor Registration, where we'll attempt some 'website scraping' – collecting data such as names and email address that are displayed on a webpage. This will be your toughest challenge yet.

Specifically, we'll cover:

- what Python is and how to use it;
- using variables, loops and if statements in Python;
- more advanced features such as lists and Regular Expressions; and
- extracting data from webpages.

How do we get started with Python?

Unfortunately, Python is not quite as easy to get started with as HTML, CSS or JavaScript, as it does not run on a browser. To try it out, you have two choices – the easy way or the hard way.

The easy way

There are a number of Python interpreters that will process Python code for you on the web. In this chapter we will be using https://repl.it/languages/python3, and our advice to you would be to do the same. It requires no installation or setup, and you can get started right away. There are a number of other websites you can try which do the same thing, such as www.tutorialspoint. com/execute_python_online.php and skulpt.org.

The hard way

Another option is to install Python on your computer and run it directly from there. This has the advantage of not requiring an internet connection, and allows you to try out a full installation of Python, but it does require some trickier setup. We would recommend against this method unless you are a fairly advanced computer user.

If you'd like to try this way, you can download Python at www. python.org/downloads/ (choose the latest version 3 available). You only need to do this on Windows – most OSX and Linux machines come with Python built in.

Once Python is installed, you will need to create a text file called, for example, mypython.py. You can do that in your text editor using File → Save As.

You will then need to open up a command line window, which you can do by typing cmd in the search box on Windows, or opening the Terminal app in OSX.

You can then run the Python script using the command:

```
python mypython.py
```

This will then display the output of your script. You can also just type:

```
python
```

to be able to run individual Python commands.

If you have problems with this method, there are a number of online guides to help you getting started with Python, or you can just use the easy way recommended above.

'Visitor Registration' with Python

Now that we are up and running with Python, let's run a basic script. If you are using the easy method, when you go to https://repl.it/languages/python3 you should see this screen (6.2):

6.2

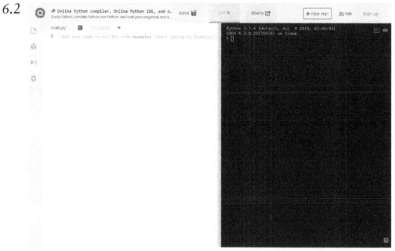

Here, you can enter your Python code on the left and click the 'run' button to see the output in the box on the right. If you make something you are particularly proud of, you can share or save your work too.

Our first Python script will simply output the words 'Welcome to Coding Solutions Enterprises'. To do that, enter this code on the left and click the 'run' button.

```
print("Welcome to Coding Solutions Enterprises")
```

This will give you this output (6.3):

6.3

So what does 'print' do? Unlike JavaScript, with Python we don't have a webpage to interact with, or to 'alert' our information to the user. Instead, we have something called the *console*. This is used in most programming languages (there is actually one in JavaScript as well) and it's a space for developers to view the output of their code.

The console is often used when debugging, to allow us to check the values of variables for example, and we'll be using it here to see what our program is doing.

So print("Welcome to Coding Solutions Enterprises") prints those welcome words to the console, ie the black box on the right. Simple as that!

Variables in Python

In JavaScript we used 'var' to create a variable. In Python we just define the variable like this:

```
name = "Rob"
```

This will create a variable called 'name' with a value of 'Rob'.

Challenge 1

Create a variable with a value of your name and then print it to the console.

Solution: Your code should look like this:

```python
name = "Rob"
print(name)
```

Notice that we use print(name), not print("name"), because 'name' is a variable name, not a value.

6.4

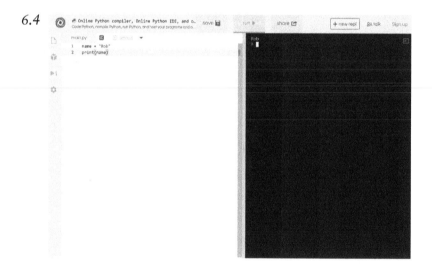

We can combine strings with a +, just like in JavaScript. Try changing your code to output our welcome message followed by your name (6.5):

6.5

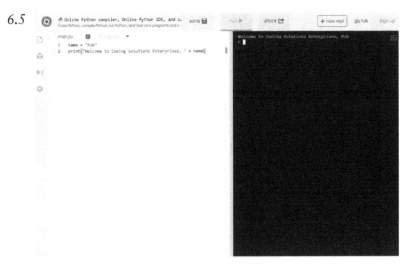

Boolean variables

Like many other languages, JavaScript includes *Boolean varia-bles*. Named after George Boole, an English mathematician who specialized in logic, they can only take the values true or false.

You might want to use them to check if a user is already registered as a guest, for example. You would create the variable in the normal way:

```
isRegistered = True
```

You could then use *if statements*, covered later on in the chapter, to test whether or not the user is already registered.

Lists

Lists are similar to variables but they allow us to store many values in one object. When you are viewing your inbox, for example, your email app can't create a differently named variable to contain the content for each email. Instead, programmers use lists. Lists are also known as arrays in other languages.

To create a list containing the names of visitors to our company, we would use code like this:

```
names = ["Rob", "Kirsten", "Tommy", "Ralphie"]
```

The square brackets ([and]) define a list, and then we separate the different members, or elements, of the list with commas.

We can then print the whole list using:

```
print(names)
```

and if we want to access a particular element within the list we use the square brackets again:

```
print(names[0])
```

– this would print 'Rob'. Note that the numbering for the list elements starts at 0, so names[2] would return 'Tommy'. This is easy for new programmers to forget, and a common mistake is to think that names[3] returns the third element in the list, when it is in fact the fourth.

The number of an element is known as its *index*.

To see all this in action (6.6):

6.6

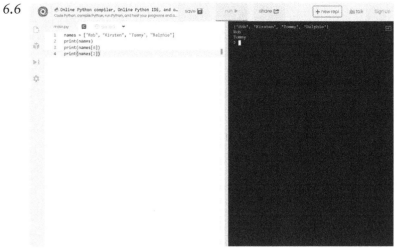

```
1  names = ["Rob", "Kirsten", "Tommy", "Ralphie"]
2  print(names)
3  print(names[0])
4  print(names[2])
```

PRACTICE EXERCISES

We might also store the types of vehicles that we saw earlier in our web application in a list.

If we create a list using the following code:

```
vehicles = ["SUV", "Saloon", "Estate", "Truck"]
```

what would be returned by:
vehicles[3]
vehicles[4]
vehicles[0]
vehicles[1] + "and" + vehicles[2]

Answers:
Truck
Nothing (this would give an error in your code)
SUV
Saloon and Estate

Manipulating lists

When working with lists, we often need to change values for elements, add elements on to the end, or remove elements. We can do all of these easily in Python.

To change an element's value, just adjust it in the usual way, for example:

```
vehicles [2] = "Station Wagon"
```

To remove an element from a list by its value, use .remove:

```
vehicles.remove("SUV")
```

Or to remove an element by its index, use .pop:

```
vehicles.pop(0)
```

To insert a value at a particular point in the list, we can use .insert, like this:

```
vehicles.insert(1, "Motorcycle")
```

– this would add 'Motorcycle' in position 1.

PRACTICE EXERCISE

Let's take an example list which contains a range of numbers.
What command (or commands) would be required to turn the list:

```
myList = [1, 2, 3, 4]
```

into:

```
[1, 2, 3]
[2, 3, 4]
[1, 2, 3, 4, 5]
[2, 2, 3, 3, 4]
```

Answers:

```
myList.remove(4) or myList.pop(3)
myList.remove(1) or myList.pop(0)
myList.insert(4, 5)
myList[0] = 2 and myList.insert(2, 3)
```

– note there are other ways to solve this one.

For loops

In the JavaScript chapter we used loops to repeat a chunk of code several times; if you recall, we used a loop to print out the parking bay numbers to the user. We can do the same thing in Python, but it looks a little different:

```
for x in range(0, 10):
    print x
```

Let's see this in action (6.7):

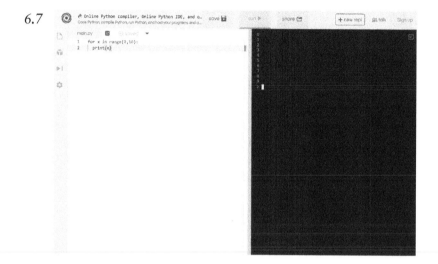

6.7

Hopefully this makes sense – range(0, 10) means loop through the whole numbers from 0 up to (but not including) 10. The : defines the beginning of the content of the loop and then x is printed each time the loop runs.

In JavaScript we used { and } to define our loop content. Here there is only a : – it is the indentation that sets the limits for the loop content.

Try some loops out for yourself:

PRACTICE EXERCISE

Use loops to display:

1 The actual parking bay numbers, ie not zero.

2 The sequence reversed, ie 10,9,8,7, etc.

Answers:

1

```
for x in range(0, 10):
    print(x+1)
```

2

```
for x in range(0, 10):
    print(10 - x)
```

For loops and lists

For loops in Python were really designed for looping through lists. Say, for example, we had a list defined which recorded the number of visitors in each of the last five days:

```
visitors = [36, 35, 25, 21, 15]
```

We could display all the elements in the list like this:

```
for total in visitors:
    print(total)
```

6.8

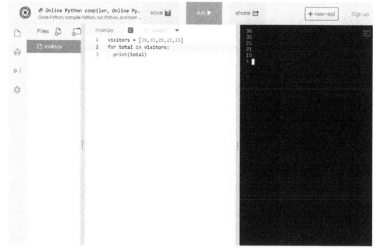

Later on we might have a requirement to add in an additional five occasional workers who, although strictly not visitors, may need to be added to the daily totals for reporting purposes. We could do it manually, but it would be much neater to do it with a loop. To do this we need to know the *index* of each item in the array (remember the index of the first item in the array is 0, the second is 1, etc).

We can't get that with our current for loop, so we need a different approach. Instead of looping through the array, we loop through the *indexes*, starting at 0, and going up to one less than the number of items in the list. We can get the number of items in the list, or the *length* of the list, using the *len* command:

```
print(len(visitors))
```

In our case, this returns 5 (6.9):

6.9

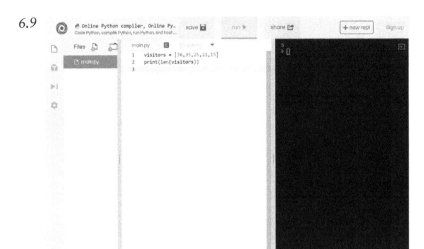

So we can use a range to loop through the list indexes. Remember that range(0, 10) loops through the numbers 0 to 9, so range(0, len(visitors)) will loop through each of the list indexes.

Finally then we can solve the problem of adding five occasional workers to each value in the list:

```python
visitors = [36, 35, 25, 21, 15]
for i in range(0, len(visitors)):
    visitors[i] = visitors[i] + 5
print(visitors)
```

This code loops through the numbers 0, 1, 2, 3 and 4, and then adds 5 to the list values in each case. You can see the result on the right below, as each of the values is increased by 5 (6.10):

6.10

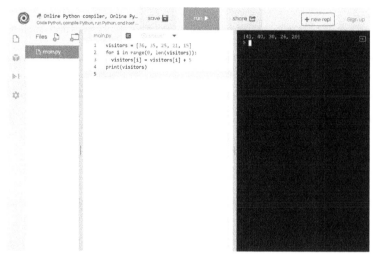

PRACTICE EXERCISES

Create a list containing any five numbers, and then loop through the array, doubling each number. Finally print the output to the console.

Answer:

```
numbers = [10, 20, 30, 40, 50]
for i in range(0, len(numbers)):
    numbers[i] = numbers[i] * 2
print(numbers)
```

6.11

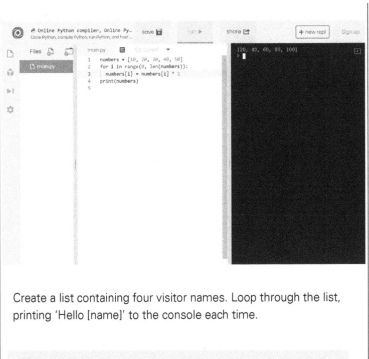

Create a list containing four visitor names. Loop through the list, printing 'Hello [name]' to the console each time.

```python
names = ["John", "Paul", "Ringo", "George"]
for name in names:
    print("Hello " + name)
```

Answer:

6.12

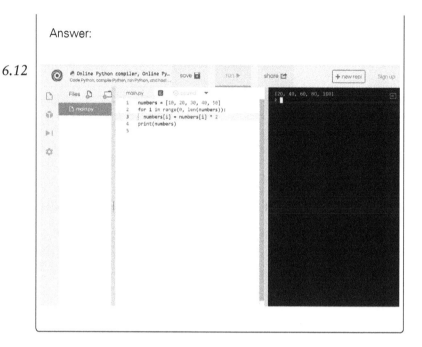

While loops

Just like in JavaScript, in Python we can use while loops as well as for loops. They work like this:

```
i = 0
while (i < 10):
        print(i)
        i = i + 1
```

We start off by setting the variable 'i' to 0, and then as with JavaScript we keep going as long as i is less than 10, adding one to i each time the loop is processed. The output is the numbers 0 to 9, as you can see below (6.13):

6.13

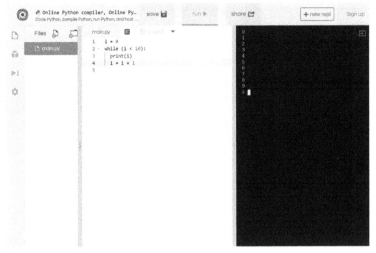

Challenge 2

Use a while loop to display the visitor parking bays from 10 to 1 in descending order as before.

This one just requires a bit of tweaking to the above example – start off by setting i to 10, and then change the while condition and the final instruction so that i decreases by one each time, until i is 1.

```
i = 10
while (i >= 1):
        print(i)
        i = i - 1
```

And here it is in action (*6.14*):

6.14

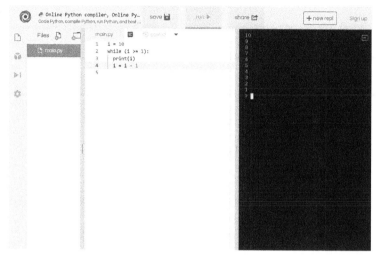

As in the practice exercise, create a list containing four visitor names. We're now going to use a while loop to complete the challenge. Loop through the list, printing 'Hello [name]' to the console each time.

This time we are using a while loop to cycle through the contents of a list. The process is fairly straightforward, setting i to 0 initially and then keeping going as long as i is less than the length of the array. Here is the code:

```
names = ["John", "Paul", "Ringo", "George"]
i = 0
while (i < len(names)):
        print("Hello " + names[i])
        i = i + 1
```

6.15

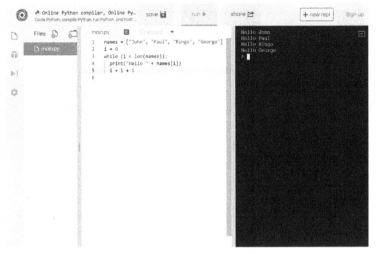

If statements

If statements work in much the same way as with JavaScript. Say a visitor regularly visits the company and you want to test whether the number of visits is greater than 100. We might wish to reward a loyal visitor/customer with a complimentary coffee or perhaps a discount. To do this you would use this code:

```
visits = 120
if visits > 100:
        print("Welcome, you have visited over 100
    times! - You are entitled to a 10% discount on our
    services.")
```

6.16

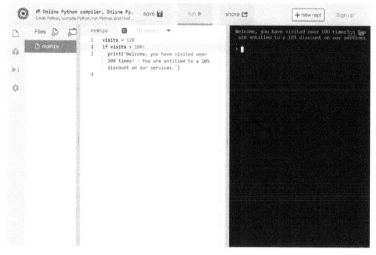

Try changing the value of 'visits' to see how this affects the output.

We can add an 'else' option as well, to run some code if the statement is not true – in this case a standard welcome message:

```
visits = 80
if visits > 100:
    print('Welcome, you have visited over 100 times! -
  You are entitled to a 10% discount on our services.')
else:
  print("Welcome to Coding Solutions Enterprises")
```

6.17

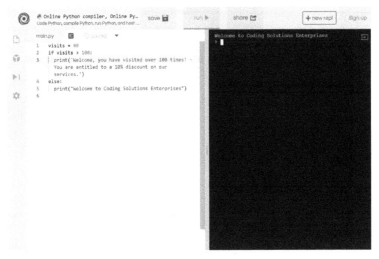

In some cases, we might want to check for two conditions to be true at once, such as the number of visits being over 100 and the time period being under, say, 365 days. We can do that using the *and operator*, which allows us to check for both conditions being true:

```python
visits = 110
period = 180
if visits > 100 and period < 365:
    print('Welcome, you have visited over 100 times! -
    You are entitled to a 10% discount on our services.')
    else:
    print("Welcome to Coding Solutions Enterprises")
```

6.18

Note: you can use the or *operator in the same way, to check for one of two (or more) conditions being true.*

We can also test for a variable being equal to another using == (as with JavaScript). We might wish to evaluate a user log on the back-end administration system for our Visitor Registration application:

```
username = "rob"
if username == "rob":
        print("Hi Rob!")
else:
        print("I don't know you")
```

6.19

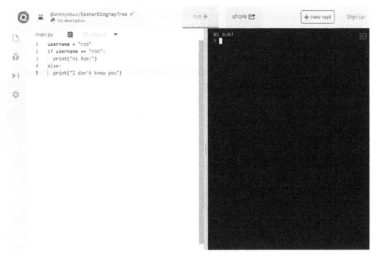

We can also use != (an exclamation mark followed by an equals sign) to test whether two variables are different.

Finally, we can use the 'elif' command to look for other conditions. Elif is short for 'else if' and allows us to combine a number of if statements. This code looks for 'rob' and then 'darren' as usernames:

```python
username = "dave"
if username == "rob":
        print("Hi Rob!")
elif username == "darren":
        print("Hi Darren!")
else:
        print("I don't know you")
```

6.20

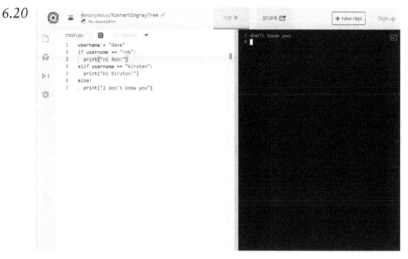

```
main.py
1   username = "dave"
2   if username == "rob":
3       print("Hi Rob!")
4   elif username == "kirsten":
5       print("Hi Kirsten!")
6   else:
7       print("I don't know you")
```

PRACTICE EXERCISES

1 Create variables called 'username' and 'password', and check for four different options:

- Username and password correct.
- Username correct and password wrong.
- Username wrong and password correct.
- Both username and password wrong.

Give the user an appropriate error message in each case.
We complete this challenge with a set of nested if statements:

```
username = "rob"
password = "myPassword"
if username == "rob" and password == "myPassword":
    print("Correct, you are logged in!")
elif username == "rob" and password != "myPassword":
    print("Your password is wrong")
```

```
elif username != "rob" and password == "myPassword":
    print("Your username is wrong")
else:
    print("Both your username and password are
wrong")
```

6.21

2 Recall our list of visitor numbers for the last 5 days. Use a combination of a for loop and an if statement to loop through the array [36,31,25,21,15] and print all the values greater than 30 visitors.

This time we have an if statement inside a for loop – it's a fairly simple setup:

```
visits = [36, 31, 25, 21, 15]
for total in visits:
    if total > 30:
            print(total)
```

6.22

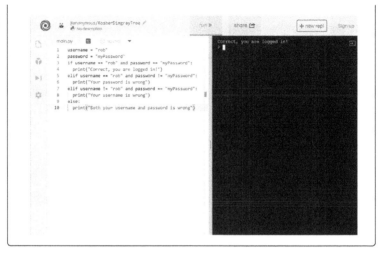

```
username = "rob"
password = "myPassword"
if username == "rob" and password == "myPassword":
    print("Correct, you are logged in!")
elif username == "rob" and password != "myPassword":
    print("Your password is wrong")
elif username != "rob" and password == "myPassword":
    print("Your username is wrong")
else:
    print("Both your username and password is wrong")
```

Challenge 3

Let's say we have an array of all the visitors over the last two days. We would perhaps expect there to be instances where the same individual has visited on more than one occasion. It would be useful to pull out only the unique visits to the organization.

This is a hard one. Loop through the array ["Rob","Kirsten", "Darren","Rafferty","Rob","Darren","Barnaby","Rob"] printing each unique visitor only once. This is harder than it seems, and will require you to create an array of the visitor names you have already printed. Feel free to glance at the solution below if you need some inspiration. Good luck!

Solution:

This is definitely the most complex code we're written so far. For each of the numbers in the List, the code loops through an 'alreadyPrintedNames' List to see if that name has already been printed. If it hasn't, the code prints the name and adds it to the 'alreadyPrintedNames' List.

```
names = ["Rob","Kirsten","Darren","Rafferty","Rob",
"Darren","Barnaby","Rob"]
alreadyPrintedNames = []
for name in names:
    alreadyPrinted = False
    for alreadyPrintedName in alreadyPrintedNames:
        if name == alreadyPrintedName:
            alreadyPrinted = True
    if alreadyPrinted == False:
        print(name)
        alreadyPrintedNames.append(name)
```

Well done if you solved this one. It wasn't easy.

6.23

Regular expressions

Regular expressions are a little tricky to get to grips with, but they are an extremely powerful way of processing text. At the end of this chapter we will be using them to get some summarized visitor data from a webpage and then process it to collect all the email addresses.

Regular expressions allow you to search through a string and extract a particular piece of information, or *substring*.

Regular expressions are our first example of code that requires a Python *module* – that is, an extra set of functions that extend Python's standard functionality.

To import the regular expressions Python module you use the code:

```
import re
```

Simple!

Now let's see it in action. Suppose you wanted to extract the name Rob from the string 'My Name is Rob.'. With regular expressions, you could do it like this:

```
import re
string = 'My Name is Rob.'
result = re.search('is (.*).', string)
print(result.group(1))
```

We start by importing the re module, and then creating our string. The next line is where the magic happens – we use the re.search function to search the string, and then we use the *regular expression* 'is (.*).' to find what we need. This expression essentially means 'return the text after "is" and before ".".'

Finally, result.group(1) gives us the text that we need. Let's see it in action (*6.24*):

Challenge 4

Use regular expressions to extract the word 'quick' from the string 'The quick brown fox'.

Solution:

The following code will do the trick:

```
import re
string = 'The quick brown fox'
result = re.search('The (.*) brown', string)
print(result.group(1))
```

Note that you could use several different strings in the regular expression. For example, 'b' and ' brown fox' would both work after the (.*). Try them out (6.25)!

6.25

Splitting strings into lists

We're getting close to being able to complete the web scraping challenge for this section. What if we had multiple bits of text that we wanted to extract from a string? For example, say we had the string 'Rob,Kirsten,Tommy,Ralphie' and wanted to extract each of the names.

It is possible to do this with regular expressions, but we'll use a different method – splitting the string into a list.

We do this with the command string.split(","), with the "," being the character we want to split the string up with.

So to split our string we would do this:

```
string = "Rob,Kirsten,Tommy,Ralphie"
print(string.split(","))
```

Note: *we don't need 'import re' for this as we are not using regular expressions.*

The result is a list containing the four names (6.26):

6.26

Challenge 5

Take the HTML '<li>John</li> <li>Paul</li> <li>George</li> <li>Ringo</li>', and split it up into the individual list items.

Solution:

Here we can use the space between each list item to split the string, so this code will do the trick:

```python
string = "<li>John</li> <li>Paul</li> <li>George</li>
<li>Ringo</li>"
print(string.split(" "))
```

See it in action (6.27):

6.27

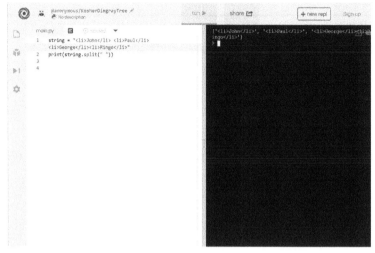

Note: we can also use just string.split() to split a string by the space character.

Challenge 6

Use regular expressions to extract and print the names from the HTML code in Chapter 1.

Once we have obtained our list, we can loop through the items, and use re.search to extract just the names:

```python
import re
string = "<li>John</li> <li>Paul</li> <li>George</li>
    <li>Ringo</li>"
namesList = string.split(" ")
for name in namesList:
    result = re.search('<li>(.*)</li>', name)
    print(result.group(1))
```

This gives us the four names (*6.28*):

6.28

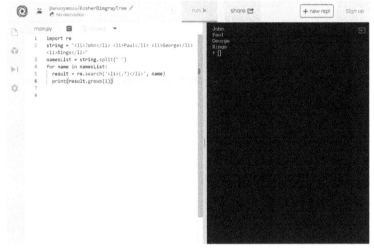

Getting the contents of a webpage

We're very close now to being able to complete our web scraping project. The one other skill we need is to be able to get the content of a webpage. This will allow us to get some data to work with to extract the information we need, such as a collection of email addresses.

To do this, we'll need to use a new Python processor, as repl.it doesn't support getting the contents of a webpage. We'll be using trinket.io, as it supports all the features we need.

Go to https://trinket.io, and sign up for a free account. Once registered we now want to start a new trinket. In the version at the time of writing, there is a Home icon in the top grey menu: click this. This will bring up your account with recent trinkets. In the top right is a blue button [New Trinket]; click this and select Python from the drop down menu. You should see something like this (*6.29*):

6.29

This is our, hopefully quite familiar, Python editor.
the code below:

```
import urllib.request
page = urllib.request.urlopen('http://www.example.com')
print(page.read())
```

This code imports the urllib.request module, which allows us to get the contents of a URL (web address). Then we 'request' the contents of www.example.com, and finally we print the output to the console.

If all goes well you should see the HTML of www.example. com in the trinket.io window (6.30):

6.30

That's it. You can now get the contents of any web address just by changing the URL in the code above. Try any web address you like (the source code for www.google.com will likely make your head spin).

Python project: extracting visitor contact data from a webpage

Hurrah! We're ready to complete the final project, which is to take the contents of a webpage and extract the contact data we need. We might envisage using this information to send important notifications to potential visitors, such as warning of inclement weather.

To keep things simple, we're going to use the data at robpercival. co.uk/sampledata.html. This is a simple table containing some names, addresses, email addresses and phone numbers. This tabled data represents information that might have been captured and stored when our visitors registered. This webpage might also be the frontend to a customer relationship management (CRM) system, or other business data source.

The challenge, and this is a big one, is to use the skills you learned in this chapter to extract the data from the table. You should create four lists, one for each of the data columns (name, address, email and phone number).

You'll need to look at the code of the website (you can do that by right-clicking on the page and selecting 'View page source' or similar). We won't give you any more hints, but if you get stuck just glance at the solution below.

Good luck!

Solution

Did you manage it? We hope so. Here we're going to work through the solution to show you how we would have solved it.

First, we need to get the contents of the URL. We can do that using code similar to the URL-reading process that we just learned:

```
import urllib.request
page = urllib.request.urlopen('http://www.robpercival.
co.uk/sampledata.html')
print(page.read())
```

This gives us the HTML of the webpage (6.31):

6.31

You can see that the data is contained in HTML (you may want to brush up on the tables section from the HTML chapter if it's unfamiliar). The HTML chunk for each row looks like this:

```
<tr>
    <td>Moses York</td>
    <td>P.O. Box 998, 3708 Est Rd.</td>
    <td>et.magnis.dis@quamPellentesquehabitant.ca</td>
    <td>(728) 694-5147</td>
</tr>
```

To get the data we need, we are going to need to split up each of the rows. We can do that using string.split, like this:

```
import urllib.request
page = urllib.request.urlopen('http://www.robpercival.
co.uk/sampledata.html')
string = page.read()
rowList = string.split("<tr>")
print(rowList)
```

6.32

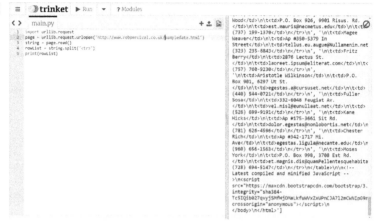

We now have a list containing the HTML for each row. If you look carefully at the HTML code, you'll see that the line breaks have been replaced with \n – this is a standard way of representing a line break in a string, both in Python and other programming languages.

Next, we need to split up each row. To do that, we'll loop through *rowList*, and split it using the '\n' symbol:

```python
import urllib.request
page = urllib.request.urlopen('http://www.robpercival.
co.uk/sampledata.html')
string = page.read()
rowList = string.split("<tr>")
for row in rowList:
    rowContentList = row.split("\n")
    print(rowContentList)
```

We now have each row as its own list (*6.33*):

6.33

Our final step is to extract the data that we need. We'll do this using re.search:

```python
import urllib.request
import re
page = urllib.request.urlopen('http://www.robpercival.
co.uk/sampledata.html')
string = page.read()
rowList = string.split("<tr>")
for row in rowList:
        rowContentList = row.split("\n")
        for lineOfHTML in rowContentList:
                if "<td>" in lineOfHTML:
                        s = re.search("<td>(.*)</td>",
lineOfHTML)
                        print(s.group(1))
```

(Don't forget the import re!)

In the last three lines, we test to see if there is a <td>in the line of HTML (because we are only interested in the data items, which are the lines with a <td>in them), and if there is we extract the data using re.search.

This gives the following output (6.34):

6.34

```
≡  🔵trinket  ▶ Run  ▼  ? Modules

< >    main.py                                        + ± 🖼
    1  import urllib.request
    2  import re
    3  page = urllib.request.urlopen('http://www.robpercival.co.uk/sampledata.html')
    4  string = page.read()
    5  rowList = string.split("<tr>")
    6 ▾ for row in rowList:
    7      rowContentList = row.split("\n")
    8 ▾    for lineOfHTML in rowContentList:
    9 ▾        if "<td>" in lineOfHTML:
   10              s = re.search("<td>(.*)</td>", lineOfHTML)
   11              print(s.group(1))
```

```
Plato Wood
P.O. Box 926, 9901 Risus. Rd.
est.mauris@necmetus.edu
(737) 199-1370
Magee Weaver
Ap #350-5379 In Street
tellus.eu.augue@Nullamenim.net
(323) 235-6843
Fritz Berry
2876 Lectus St.
laoreet.ipsum@eliterat.com
(757) 760-9230
Aristotle Wilkinson
P.O. Box 901, 6297 Ut St.
egestas.a@cursuset.net
(440) 544-0721
Fuller Sosa
332-6048 Feugiat Av.
vel.nisl@eunullaat.net
(526) 699-9191
Kane Hicks
Ap #175-3661 Sit Rd.
dolor.egestas@nonlobortis.net
(781) 626-4596
Chester Rich
Ap #342-1717 Mi. Ave
egestas.ligula@necante.edu
(960) 656-1563
Moses York
P.O. Box 998, 3708 Est Rd.
et.magnis.dis@quamPellentesquehabitant.ca
(728) 694-5147
```

We've done it. Congratulations if you managed to do all of that yourself – it was not a simple problem. For this challenge we had to use a range of programming techniques such as loops and if statements, as well as lists and variables. We also imported two Python modules and used regular expressions to extract data from a website. Not bad!

Summary

We are now going to apply the skills we have learned in the world of Web and app development. However, if you want to spend more time with Python, there are plenty of free resources available, some of which are listed below.

Further learning

- www.codecademy.com/courses/introduction-to-python-6WeG3/ (archived at https://perma.cc/RSJ6-TE6U) – interactive Python lessons.
- www.tutorialspoint.com/python/ (archived at https://perma.cc/JBK8-36LJ) – free Python tutorials.
- https://play.google.com/store/apps/details?id=com.sololearn.python&hl=en_GB (archived at https://perma.cc/FM9J-WQX6) – Android app for learning Python.
- https://itunes.apple.com/gb/app/learn-python-pro/id953972812?mt=8 (archived at https://perma.cc/PZ3V-AF8D) – iPhone and iPad app for learning Python.

PART THREE

In practice

## CHAPTER SEVEN

Website development

Our first look at coding in practice will be to learn how we can build and share a website with the world. A website is probably the simplest thing you can build with code, and yet it can be hugely powerful. The potential to create something in a few minutes that anyone in the world can access is quite intoxicating – yet if you've worked through the previous chapters in this book you already know how to do just that.

We'll start by seeing how the coding world has transitioned from software that runs on a 'local' computer (ie the machine sitting on your desk or lap) to websites, which primarily run on a 'remote' computer, connected to your PC or phone via the internet.

Next, we'll consider the reasons why a non-web developer might want to build a website, whether it's for career advancement, pleasure or creating an online presence.

We'll then look at three options for creating a website: using a service such as Weebly or Squarespace, hosting your own using a content management system such as Wordpress, and finally coding the site yourself from scratch. You'll learn the advantages and disadvantages of all three, and find out which option to use depending on the nature of the site you want to build.

Finally, we'll look at one of the most popular frameworks for building great looking sites, Bootstrap, and in the closing project for this section we'll make a simple website.

By the end of this section, you will be familiar with the different ways that you can create and host websites, and be ready to build one for any project or business that you want to start.

Why build a website?

A hundred years ago, if you wanted to start a business, you would likely have needed a great deal of capital. At the least you would have needed premises to sell your goods, staff to make your product or financing for raw materials.

All that has changed in the last 20 years, where some of the most valuable businesses in the world exist purely online, and were created by individuals with almost zero initial costs. Learning to code gives you the power to put any idea you have into action while investing no more than your time and the price of a few cups of coffee. You don't even need to ask anyone for permission!

But even if you don't want to start a business, there are many other reasons you might want to build your own website.

A blog is a great way to build a name for yourself online. You can share your love of dogs, your horticultural knowledge, or even document the process of learning to code. Write well and you can create a community of like-minded individuals, and you never know what opportunities might come out of that.

If there is an online task that you do regularly, you might well be able to automate it with a website, and if other people do similar tasks, you can share your tools with them. The web scraping code we learned in the Python chapter, for example, could be used to check when prices on Amazon are updated. You could then allow your users to check the prices of particular products, and email them when they go below a particular threshold.

We will look at ways to build specific types of sites later on in the book, but for now it would be worth having a particular website in mind that you would like to build. It doesn't have to be a world-changing idea, just a particular idea that will help you apply what you learn in this chapter.

Take a few moments now and jot down this idea. Then, as you are reading through this chapter, think about how the different approaches could work with that idea, and which you would choose. If you really want to solidify your learning, create that website when you've got to the end of the chapter.

How do websites work?

The BBC Microcomputer Rob grew up with in the early 1990s was a stand-alone machine. You could add programs (software) to it via tapes and discs, but all the code was run completely on the device itself.

As the internet grew and became faster, it began to be feasible for the code for programs (now called websites) to be stored on powerful computers called servers which would then be transferred to the user's computer and displayed in a special piece of software called a browser. Initially most of these websites were static, displaying information coded using HTML and CSS.

Gradually websites became more interactive, and rather than displaying static content they allowed users to post updates, send email or even watch video. These type of sites were initially known as 'webapps', although the word has mostly gone out of usage nowadays, becoming synonymous with websites themselves. Most of the actual running of the webapp is done on the server, and the browser just displays the output (a list of the user's emails, or pictures of the user's cat for example).

The great advantage of working in this way is speed of development. On Rob's BBC Microcomputer, if he wanted an updated piece of software he had to go and get the disc for it, and put it in his machine. Now, conversely, if Google want to update the Gmail interface, or if you want to edit your blog, a quick change on the server and the website is updated immediately for all its users around the world.

Even traditional desktop software such as word processors and image editors are starting to find homes on the web and some computers, such as Chromebooks, are little more than browsers and an internet connection.

So how do we take advantage of this phenomenon? We know how to write HTML code, now we need to know how to share our code with the world. It's actually pretty simple, and requires two things: a domain name, and some web hosting.

What is a domain name, and how do I get one?

A domain name is simply a web address, like facebook.com or bbc.co.uk. Each country's domain names are managed by a central 'registrar', and domain names can be bought from a number of different providers.

When you buy a domain name, you're actually just renting it, with the average cost being around £10 per year. Once you have bought it, you have the right to renew it each year, but if you leave it unrenewed, it will eventually return to the public 'pot' and someone else can buy it.

A quick web search for 'buy domain name' will turn up several results, so do a bit of research and choose a provider that suits you. Ideally check reviews and don't decide completely on price – a cheap domain name might come with nasty fees, for example to transfer it elsewhere.

Choosing a domain name can be difficult, as most of the good ones are already gone. Domain names are very much a matter of personal preference, but we would recommend the following:

- Get a .com or a country-specific domain (like .co.uk) if at all possible. Even if it is not an ideal domain name, it will likely be more memorable and trustworthy than a more obscure extension such as .boats or .black.
- Make it easy to type. Avoid mis-spellings like Xpress (unless they are part of your brand of course!).
- Use keywords. If you want to rank highly in search engines, putting your search terms in your domain name is a great start. If you are starting a blog about cocker spaniels for example, cockerspanielsblog.com wouldn't be a bad choice (and at the time of writing this book, is available!).

If you're struggling to find ideas, these sites might help:

- www.domainsbot.com/ – will search a range domain domains and tell you which are available.
- www.namemesh.com/ – will combine two or three words and show you a range of available domain names.
- www.panabee.com/ – will suggest company names and domain names based on your keywords.

Once you have decided on a domain name, you can purchase it (perhaps start with just one year, unless you're feeling confident!) with your chosen provider, and move on to the second requirement: web hosting.

What is web hosting, and how do I get it?

When a user visits your website, the files are downloaded from a server and displayed in the user's browser. If you have a more advanced site that allows interaction with the user (such as a login or search box), the server will also run the code to provide the user with the data they need. You may also use other features associated with a domain name, such as personalized email addresses. Web hosting is the server space and computational power that manages all of this for you.

There are several different options of web hosting, depending on how much you want to pay, ease of use, and how much control you want over the content and layout of your site. We will look at the two main options for those starting out: website builders and shared hosting.

Website builders

Website builders are the simplest and quickest way to get a website up and running. Once you sign up with a company, you can choose from a range of templates and styles, and edit your site in a drag-and-drop interface.

Website builders range from $7 to $20 per month, depending on features, and some even give you the ability to create an online store, blog or portfolio site in just a few clicks.

However, there are a few major drawbacks to using these sites. First, you don't own your content. If you decide you want to move to another provider (perhaps because you need a feature that your chosen website builder doesn't support), you will have to recreate your website from scratch. Also, your ability to customize your website is often limited to what the website builder provides – you don't have the freedom to write your own code to make your site do exactly what you want. And as a coder, you'll definitely want that freedom.

For those reasons, website builders are great for getting a site up and running very quickly, but we wouldn't recommend them for a serious site that you want to own and customize to your heart's content. That method is what we will be focusing on for the rest of this section.

Nonetheless, if you'd like to try a website builder, some of the most popular providers are:

- www.weebly.com/
- www.wix.com/
- www.squarespace.com/
- www.shopify.com/

Shared hosting

If you're just starting out with a small site, and want more freedom and ownership than website builders provide, shared hosting is probably the best solution for you. To have a website, you need a hosting account with a provider to contain your website files, emails and databases. Shared hosting is when several different hosting accounts are stored on a single server. This is a very efficient way of hosting websites, and as a result it is extremely cheap. Expect to pay around $4–10 per month for a hosting package.

The big advantage of shared hosting over website builders is that you completely own your content – you can download your site from the server and switch to another provider if you wish. You also have complete control of the code for your site, so what your site can do is limited only by your imagination.

As with domain names, a quick web search for 'web hosting' will turn up a huge range of websites, and the choice can be confusing. Here are a few tips to help you choose the right provider:

- Test out their support. Send them a couple of quick questions before you sign up, such as 'How many email addresses do I get with the Starter package', and see how quickly they come back to you.
- Check reviews on sites like trustpilot.com.

- Know your needs – if you're planning on building a small site, you likely will need something like this:
  - 500MB webspace (this is hard drive space to store your website files);
  - 1GB bandwidth (this is the amount of content that is transferred from the server to your users' computers);
  - 1–5 email addresses;
  - a database;
  - one-click-installs for commonly used software such as Wordpress (we'll learn about Wordpress in a moment).
- Avoid going on price alone – you will almost certainly need some support, and you'll want fast, reliable hardware. You're unlikely to get those with the cheapest providers.

A final thought – you will likely be able to buy a domain name and web hosting from the same provider. This can be very convenient as you will have everything in one place. However, some people like to use different providers so that if they have problems with the web host, for example, that does not affect their domain names. It's a personal decision, but we would recommend using different providers to avoid having all your eggs in one basket.

I've got my web hosting, now what?

Hopefully by now you're clear on what you need, and perhaps have even purchased a domain name and set up your web hosting. What now?

First, it's worth checking if your web hosting provider has any getting started guides. These will introduce you to their control panel, and show you how to do basic things such as setting up email addresses and uploading files. The instructions for this will vary between providers, so we won't go through those here.

Once you have your web hosting, however, you have two main options for getting your site up and running: hand-coding or using a content management system.

Content management systems

A content management system (CMS) is a piece of software that you install on your web hosting to allow you to customize and manage your website. It's a bit like having a website builder, but you still own all of the content.

By far the most popular content management system is Wordpress. It was developed as a blogging platform in 2003, but now forms the CMS for over 25 per cent of all websites – that's a lot of websites.

Because it is so widely used, Wordpress has a huge range of themes and plugins available for it, many of them free. It's also completely free and open source, and you can edit the code of your site as much as you need to. We have built many Wordpress sites, and would thoroughly recommend it to build almost any site.

Getting started with Wordpress

There is not room in this book for a full Wordpress tutorial, but the following steps should be enough to get you started.

1. ONE CLICK INSTALL

Your web hosting provider should have an icon in your control panel which will allow you to install Wordpress very easily. If you can't find it, contact them and ask for instructions.

Once Wordpress is installed, you'll be taken to the Wordpress dashboard. This is where you can create and edit pages for your site, as well as write blog posts, if you are using your site as a blog. You can also manage every other aspect of your site from here. Try clicking around the left-hand menu, and you'll quickly see how to make changes and add and manage website content.

If you hover over the 'home' icon in the top left of the screen and click 'Visit Site' you'll see the default website that you have created. It will look something like this (7.1):

7.1

Confident Coding Demo Site
Just another WordPress site

Hello world!

Search...

29th August 2016
1 Comment
Edit

Welcome to WordPress. This is your first post. Edit or delete it, then start writing!

RECENT POSTS
· Hello world!

RECENT COMMENTS

Nothing much to look at right now. So probably the first change you will want to make is to install a theme to improve the look of your site.

2. CHOOSING A THEME

Wordpress has a huge range of free themes available. You can view and search them within your dashboard by clicking Appearance → Themes →Add New. When you find one you like, just click Install and then Activate, and then reload your site to see the theme in action. Note that your site probably won't look exactly like the theme image – you'll have to add the content, and perhaps change some settings in the Customiser menu (Appearance → Customise).

Sometimes, however, a free theme won't provide the quality look you are going for. In that case, it's well worth considering purchasing a premium theme. Generally, premium themes offer a better, more flexible design, as well as direct support if you have any problems with the theme. For $30–60, it can be a very sensible investment. Some of the most popular sites for finding premium themes are:

· https://themeforest.net/category/wordpress
· www.themecircle.net/

- www.templatemonster.com/wordpress-themes.php
- www.elegantthemes.com/

Once you have installed your theme and are happy with it, check out the Customiser to make it look perfect for your site, and then start adding content.

3. USING PLUGINS

Another great advantage of using Wordpress is that if there is any extra functionality you want for your site, there is almost certainly a plugin available to do it, and most of them are completely free.

You can add a new plugin by clicking Plugins → Add New and search for a plugin that does what you want. The plugin search doesn't always return the best results, so we normally do a Google search for 'Wordpress plugin [what we want the plugin to do]', and once chosen, search for it by name in the dashboard.

Plugins allow you to add simple things such as contact forms and Google maps to your sites, as well as transforming your site into a social network, or an ecommerce platform, so they are well worth investigating.

Self-coding your site

You might be wondering why we've left the option of building a website from scratch until last, especially in a book such as this. It's simply because if you want to get a website up and running quickly, usually the best way to do that is to use some kind of CMS, such as Wordpress.

Having said that, if you want to avoid the setup and complications that come with a CMS you might well want to build your site from scratch. This will give you complete control over the site content, as well as teaching you how websites function from the ground up.

So here we'll start by uploading a very simple site, adding some HTML to it, and finally we'll see how to use a framework such as Bootstrap to make our website look great on a range of screen sizes (this is known as building a responsive website).

Editing the index.html file for your site

Your web hosting control panel should include a file manager, allowing you to access and edit your files. Access the file manager, and find a folder with a name like 'public_html'. This is where your website files should be stored (if you have problems finding the folder, contact your web hosting provider).

Once you have found the public website folder, look for a file called index.html. If it's not there, create it in the file manager. Then edit it (again, you should be able to do this in the file manager).

Add the following code:

```
<h1> Hello World </h1>
```

Then save the file and open up your domain name in a browser. You should see something like this (7.2):

7.2

Hello World

Hurrah! Your HTML page is now available for all the world to see. Of course, you can now use any of the HTML, CSS and JavaScript that you have learned and put it in that file to customize your webpage.

Using FTP to manage your website files

You might be thinking that building a complex site by typing code into a file manager would be a bit of a hassle, and you'd be quite right. Every time you want to edit your site, you'd have to log in to your control panel, open the file manager, find the file, open the edit window and get to work.

A better way to interact with your files is via FTP, or File Transfer Protocol. FTP allows you to connect to your website files and upload, download and edit files directly. It's much more convenient than using a file manager.

You should be able to get your FTP settings from your web hosting provider, and once you have them, all you need is an FTP program. There are several free options, including:

- https://filezilla-project.org/ – Windows, Mac and Linux.
- www.smartftp.com/ – Windows only.
- www.coreftp.com/ – Windows only.
- https://cyberduck.io/ – Mac only.

However, our FTP program of choice is FireFTP, which is an add-on for the Mozilla Firefox browser. It works on any plat-form, and is very easy to use. To get it, you'll need to first download Firefox at www.firefox.com and then download FireFTP from http://fireftp.net/

Once those are installed, you'll need to enter your FTP login details, click OK and then click Connect. If all goes well (and you can contact your web hosting provider if it doesn't) you'll see a list of the files on your server, and you can navigate to the public_html folder to see your website files.

Once you see the index.html file, you can right-click on it and select 'Open' to edit it directly in your text editor.

Alternatively, you can download it to your computer, edit it there, and then upload it again when you are finished.

Using a web framework

You have probably noticed that the websites we've built so far have not been beautiful. We focused primarily on the content, and let the browser choose how to display it. This leaves us with webpages that are functional, but look like they were built in the 1990s.

If you are a great designer, you can customize the look of your site to your heart's content. However, for most of us, a quick solution to this is to use a web framework, which is essentially a collection of CSS and JavaScript which make our websites look better.

Frameworks also allow our website to be responsive, that is to adjust itself to display differently on different screen sizes and devices. This is very important as over half of all web browsing is now done from mobile devices. We'll see how that works in a moment.

There are a number of frameworks available, including:

- http://foundation.zurb.com/
- http://firezenk.github.io/zimit/
- http://ink.sapo.pt/
- www.99lime.com/elements/

Feel free to check out the sites to see what they offer, but we'll be focusing on the most popular web framework, Bootstrap.

Bootstrap was built by two Twitter employees, but has since taken on a life of its own, with over 15 per cent of the top million websites currently using it. You can see it in action at http://getbootstrap.com.

Setup instructions for bootstrap are at https://getbootstrap.com/docs/5.3/getting-started/introduction/, but the quickest way to get started is to copy the code at http://robpercival.co.uk/bootstrap.html into your index.html file and see it in action.

The demo page looks like this (7.3):

7.3

Rather nicer than our plain HTML pages. All of the standard HTML features such as forms, buttons and even plain text look more attractive and are easier to work with than before.

If you look through the HTML of the page, you'll see that there are links to the Bootstrap CSS in the header, and then some JavaScript at the bottom of the code, which is what creates the look and layout of the page.

How about the responsiveness? Try changing the width of your browser window, and you'll see that the content automatically adjusts (7.4):

This works using breakpoints: the site detects the width of the user's screen and displays the content appropriately.

There is a huge amount you can do with Bootstrap, and there is not the space to cover it here, but the main website http:// getbootstrap.com has a huge range of examples and guides to get you started.

If you want to learn bootstrap, our advice is simply to start building a site with it and use the docs to figure it out as you go along.

7.4

Heading

Donec id elit non mi porta gravida at eget metus. Fusce dapibus, tellus ac cursus commodo, tortor mauris condimentum nibh, ut fermentum massa justo sit amet risus. Etiam porta sem malesuada magna mollis euismod. Donec sed odio dui.

Website development project: build a website

That brings us to the end of this section, and there's a pretty obvious challenge for you – build a website. Whether it be a Wordpress blog documenting your love for My Little Ponies, a Weebly shop selling your homemade trinkets or a self-coded Facebook killer, build something and share it with the world.

Whether or not your site is successful is not the point here – the purpose of the challenge is to turn a goal into a reality, and learn about how websites work while you're doing it.

Good luck, and send Rob the results of your hard work on Twitter at @techedrob. We look forward to seeing what you create!

Summary

In this chapter our aim was to go from some knowledge of HTML, CSS and JavaScript, to creating and sharing a real website with the world. We considered several reasons you might want to build a site, and how websites are different to software. Then we learned about domain names and web hosting, and the different ways you can get your website live. Finally, we saw how we can use CMSs such as Wordpress and frameworks like Bootstrap to get great looking, responsive websites up and running fast.

We're now going to move away from websites and see how we can use our coding skills to build apps for mobile devices, starting with iPhones and iPads. It's a very different process to working with websites, but many of the principles are the same. Apps represent a whole new way to get our content in the hands of users, and it's pretty simple to get started, so let's go!

Further learning

As well as the recommendations from the previous chapters to learn HTML, CSS, JavaScript and Python, there are holistic courses available to teach you every aspect of web development.

- www.udemy.com/the-complete-web-developer-course-2/ (archived at https://perma.cc/7EB2-ABGA) – The Complete Web Developer Course (by Rob) uses projects and real-life exercises to teach every aspect of web development.
- www.open.ac.uk/courses/modules/tt284 (archived at https://perma.cc/EP6B-S2ME) – Open University course covering the foundations of web technologies and developing applications.
- www.theodinproject.com/courses/web-development-101 (archived at https://perma.cc/5ECT-SN9X) – A free and open-source online course in web development.

## CHAPTER EIGHT

Building an app for iPhone or iPad

Now that you have seen how to build and host complete websites, we are going to learn how to build apps that can run natively on the iPhone and iPad. Barely a week goes by without a news story of the latest app craze that is sweeping the nation (at the time of writing it's Mario Kart Tour), and the exciting thing for coders is that quite often successful apps are built by individuals or small groups rather than big companies.

Moreover, the best apps often do one thing very well – they don't need to be hugely complex. For example, Pocket, developed by Nate Weiner in 2007 after teaching himself to code, lets people save articles on the web to read later. It now has over 22 million users and has raised over $7.5million in investment.

In this section, we'll see how to make a basic Visitor Registration iPhone app to complement the webpage we've been working on. We will run it on a simulator within your computer. We'll add user interface elements like labels and buttons, and write some code in Swift, the Apple-designed language used for iPhone app development.

A word of warning – the software required to create iPhone apps can only be run on a Mac, so if you don't have one you'll need to get hold of one to start building iPhone apps. We would recommend borrowing a MacBook from a friend for a week or so, and if you enjoy the app-making process consider investing in an Apple laptop yourself. Alternatively, you can jump to the next section, Android app development, which can be done on any platform – Windows, Mac or Linux.

What is an app?

This may seem like a rather stupid question, but it's worth being clear how an app is different to a website. As we've seen, a website is stored on a server, and is then downloaded by your computer or phone and displayed in a browser. An app is different, in that the code for the app is stored on your device, meaning that it can run completely offline.

Having said that, apps often have an online component, enabling them to provide services such as messaging or getting information like weather updates.

So while websites are stored on servers and are downloaded to the users' device, apps are stored on the device themselves. This is close to the original software model where all our software was stored locally on our computer.

In this section we'll be making apps for iOS, which is the operating system that runs on iPhones and iPads.

Getting started: downloading Xcode

Making an app is often seen as a mysterious process that only expert coders can do, but it's actually very simple. All you need to build an iPhone (or iPad) app is a Mac, and a copy of Xcode, a free piece of software made by Apple.

To download Xcode, go to the App Store or to https://developer. apple.com/download/. You'll need to create an Apple developer account if you don't already have one, but this is completely free and only requires you to enter your email address and a few other details.

Once you've logged on, make sure that the Release tab is selected and download the latest version of Xcode. You will be redirected to the App Store to launch the download. It's a big file (around 7.5 GB), so depending on your internet connection you might want to go and have a cup of tea while you wait.

When it's downloaded, simply click on the downloaded file to start the installation process. This normally takes several minutes, and when it's done you should be presented with a start-up screen (if you don't see a screen that asks you choose a template for your app, open up the Xcode application and click File → New → Project in the menu at the top left of the screen).

The app setup process

We will now be presented with two screens, which allow us to choose various options for our app. In the first screen, we get to pick from several templates for our app. Make sure iOS is selected underneath 'Choose a template for your new project' and then select 'Single View App'. This will create an app with a single blank page (known in app development as a 'view') for us to edit.

You can see several other app templates, such as Game and Master-Detail App. Feel free to try them out and run them to see what they do, but we'll be sticking with the Single View App here.

Click Next, and you'll see the options screen:

· First, fill in the Product Name – you can put anything you like here, but we recommend something like 'Registration App'.

- Under Organization Name, you can put either your company or your own name.
- The Organization Identifier is like a domain name in reverse – choose something like com.yourname.
- The name and identifier are only used if you submit your app to the app store, so you can really choose anything you want at this point.
- For the user interface, make sure to select Storyboard.

The language setting can be left at the default value. We will be making use of Swift as the development language.

Click Next and you'll be asked where to save your project, so choose a suitable location, such as your Documents folder, and click Create.

After a few moments, you'll see the Xcode interface, and your app will have been created – congratulations!

The Xcode interface

This is our basic Xcode screen, and it's worth taking a few moments to familiarize yourself with it.

Underneath the usual File, Edit... menu we have the top bar, with a 'Play' button at the top left, which will allow us to run our app. Give it a try. After 30 seconds or so, you should see a small blank screen pop up. Not the most exciting app in the world – it's just a blank screen – but it's a start. This is the simulator, which enables us to try out our app without a real iPhone.

You can actually use it just like an iPhone – try clicking Hardware →Home, and you'll see the familiar iPhone home screen and you can interact with it just as you would a normal phone. Have a play around with it, and then come back to the tour.

At the right of the top bar there are several buttons which we can use to customize the interface:

- The plus button displays the Library, which presents a list of objects depending on the file we are working on. This list is empty at the moment.

- The three rectangles on the right allow us to toggle the left, bottom and right panes. Try them out!
- The double arrow displays the Code Review editor, which we won't be using here.

On to the main part of the screen:

- The left pane shows a list of the files that make up our app. We'll be looking at those in more detail shortly.
- The central window is where we'll be doing most of our work. At the moment it is displaying some settings for our app, but we'll also use it to edit files and drag and drop buttons and labels on to our app.
- The right pane is context-sensitive: it displays different information depending on what we have selected. At the moment we don't have anything selected, so it doesn't display anything, but we will be using it a lot as we create our user interface.

Finally, if you ran the app in the simulator, you'll see the console at the bottom of the screen, and it may have some information about your app in it.

This is where we will see error messages and debugging information – it can be very useful.

That's it. You're now familiar with the Xcode interface, and we can start building our app.

Adding labels to our app

Xcode has a wonderfully simple drag and drop system to add user-interface elements to our apps. We'll start by adding some text, in the form of labels.

In the left pane, select the Main.storyboard file. You may need to use pinch-to-zoom or click the -/+ buttons to be able to see the whole rectangle on the right.

The View Controller rectangle represents our iPhone app screen, and is currently blank. Click on it, and you'll see the screen change to include more settings and control options.

If you click on the plus icon in the top right, you'll now see a list of objects that you can drag into your app. In the 'Filter' box, type 'label', and then drag the label into the iPhone screen in the central pane.

As you drag it around, you'll see dotted-blue guidelines appear, which help you position your label. Try to position it in the centre of the screen, as in the screenshot.

Now you've done that, let's run the app (the Play button in the top left, or cmd-R) and see how it looks. You should see something like this (8.1):

8.1

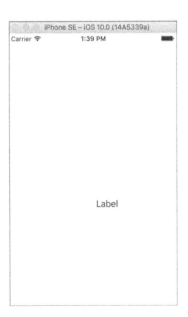

Your first non-blank iPhone app, congratulations!

(Notice that the label is not centred despite using the blue dotted lines. This is because the iPhone running in the simulator is different to the iPhone in the central pane. In our case the simulator is running an iPhone 8, and the central pane shows an iPhone 11, which is bigger. Feel free to click on the 'iPhone 8' button to change the simulator device, or the 'View as: iPhone 11' button to change the device shown in the central pane. We will use iPhone 11 for both of these from now on to keep things simple.)

Customizing the label

Now that you have added your label, make sure it is selected and then take a look at the context-sensitive right pane. It gives a list of drop-downs including text, colour and font. Most of the options are fairly self-explanatory, so try clicking on them and have a play around to see what they do.

PRACTICE EXERCISE

See if you can make your label say 'Welcome to Coding Solutions Enterprises' in pink with a green shadow.

Adding a text field

Labels are great for displaying text for the user, but they are not very interactive. To get some information from our users, we need something like a text field. Add one in the same way you added the label.

This creates a grey text field with the default iOS styling. Run the app and click in the text box, and you should be able to enter some text (8.2):

8.2

As with labels, you can customize your text field by resizing it and using the context pane on the right.

Challenge 1

Try creating this app layout (*8.3*):

8.3   Please register your visit using this app

Solution: The label is just the default size and font, and the two text boxes are aligned underneath it. You can use the 'Placeholder' setting to enter the First name and Last name text within the text fields.

Adding buttons

The final user-interface element that we will add is a button. You should be able to guess how to do this by now!

Challenge 2

Add a button, change the text to 'Register' and position it beneath the Password text field.

Running some code

That's as far as we're going to go with user interface elements. Now we're going to write some Swift code that will be processed when the app is run.

To do this, click on the ViewController.swift file in the left pane. You'll now see a page that contains some standard code for the ViewController.swift file.

The lines you'll see with // at the beginning are comments – these are notes for coders to read that are not part of the app code. They are very useful for keeping track of what certain parts of your code do (and for leaving yourself messages and reminders as you build the app).

The 'import UIKit' command imports the UIKit module, which allows us to interact with the user interface (UI).

The following line defines the ViewController class, which is essentially a chunk of code that we can use to control the view, or in other words to customize our app screen.

The 'override fun viewDidLoad()' line defines a function (also known as a method) which will be called when the app loads. This is where we will put any code that we want to run when the app is loaded.

'super.viewDidLoad()' runs some default commands to set up the view.

To write your first piece of Swift code, move the cursor underneath the 'super.viewDidLoad()' code and write the following:

```
print("This is my first piece of Swift code")
```

Run the app and see if you can spot what happened. You may have spotted that nothing happened on the app itself, but in the bottom pane in Xcode the sentence 'This is my first piece of Swift code' appeared (8.4):

8.4

That is what the print command does – it displays output in the console so we can see what our program is doing.

This is fairly useful, but really we want to use our app to display something to the user, so to do that we'll need to interact with the user interface.

Interacting with the user interface

Now we are going to use code to edit the user interface (UI). Specifically, we are going to update the main label to read 'Please register your visit using this wonderful app' instead of 'Please register your visit using this app'.

To change the UI using code, we need to create what is known as an Outlet. This is essentially a variable that we can use to refer to, for example, a label or a button. To do that, first make sure that the Main.storyboard file is selected. Then, in the top right of the central window, click the icon 'left align' and select Assistant to bring up the Assistant editor. The editor will be added to the right of the Storyboard and will display the ViewController.swift file.

Your Xcode screen should now look like this (8.5):

8.5

Now comes the tricky bit. Move the mouse to the 'Please register your visit using this app' label, press ctrl and hold on your keyboard, and then drag the mouse over to the ViewController. swift file, just underneath where it says 'class ViewController'. If all goes well you should see a window with 'connection', 'object', 'name', 'type' and 'storage' options pop up.

This allows you to create an outlet for the label. Type 'label' into the Name field (you can use a different name if you like) and click Connect. This will add the line:

```
@IBOutlet var label: UILabel!
```

to your ViewController.swift file, which will allow you to use the 'label' variable to refer to the label.

Now we just need to add our code to update the label text. Underneath your 'print' statement, add this Swift code:

```
label.text = "Please register your visit using this wonderful app"
```

As you might guess, this updates the label text to the string 'Please register your visit using this wonderful app'. Run the app and check it out. You should see this (8.6):

8.6

Please register your visit using this wonderful app

First name

Last name

Register

Hurrah! We have interaction between our code and our UI. Our next challenge is to make the button do something, so that the user can instruct the app to take some action.

Making buttons interactive

Now we will change our app so that when the user taps the 'Register' button, the words 'register' are printed to the console.

This process is similar to updating the label, but this time we will create an Action rather than an Outlet. In Xcode, ctrl-drag the button to just underneath the 'class ViewController' code, just as before. You should see the 'connection', 'object', 'name', 'type' and 'storage' popup again.

This time, click on 'Outlet' and change the option to 'Action'. Then in the Name box type buttonClicked. Click Connect and the following code will be created:

```
@IBAction func buttonClicked(_ sender: Any) {
}
```

This is a function or method that will be called when the button is clicked.

Challenge 3

Add some code to your app so that the word 'register' is printed to the console when the button is tapped.

Solution: Inside the buttonClicked method, just add the code:

```
print("register")
```

So the whole function looks like this:

```
@IBAction func buttonClicked(_ sender: Any) {

  print("register")
}
```

Now run the app and tap the button, and you should find that it works as expected.

Challenge 4

Create a new app with a label that is initially empty and a single button that says 'Register'. Then, when the button is clicked change the label text to 'Thank you for your registration!'

Solution: First click File →New→Project to create a new project and use the same settings as before. Then add a label, double click on it and press backspace to delete the text. Then add the button. Create an Outlet for the label and an Action for the button by ctrl-dragging in the same way we did previously. Finally, add the code:

```
label.text = "Thank you for your registration!"
```

to the buttonClicked() method. This should give you the following (8.7):

8.7

Run it on the simulator and the app should say 'Thank you for your registration!' when the button is tapped.

Challenge 5

Add a text field to your app with placeholder text 'Please enter your name'. Then change the code so that when the user taps the button the label text becomes 'Thank you for your registration, [user's name]!'.

Hint: You'll need to create an Outlet for the text field, and get the text field's value. You'll also need to append that to 'Thank you for your registration' to create the required string. The process for getting the text field's value is the same as for labels, and appending works the same way as in JavaScript. Xcode will give you an error message at some point – use the automatic 'fix it' command to fix the error.

Solution: Add the text field and create an Outlet for it by ctrl-dragging. We'll call it textField but you can use any variable name. Then just change the line:

```
label.text = "Thank you for your registration!"
```

to:

```
label.text = "Thank you for your registration" +
textField.text! + "!"
```

This sets the label text to a new string, equal to 'Thank you for your registration [user's name]!'. The whole app should look like this (8.8):

8.8

You are probably wondering why we need an ! after textField. text. Swift has a variable type known as an 'optional', which is a variable which could contain a null value. For example, if we created a variable like this:

```
var number:Int
```

This would create a variable called 'number' which would be an integer, but because we haven't set a value for it yet it has a 'null value' and is an optional. If we try to use it while it has a null this will cause the app to crash.

If you want to use an optional in your code you have to put an exclamation mark after it, which essentially tells the device that you are sure that it does have a value, and it is OK to use it. This is what we are doing here – putting the ! after textField.text states that we know it has a value (even if that value is an empty string) and then the app won't crash.

Optionals are quite fiddly and don't worry too much about fully understanding them at this point, but if you want to read more about them are a variety of blogs and other resources online.

Variable types in Swift

We are almost ready to build our Visitor Registration app, but we need to learn a little about variable types in Swift. In the JavaScript and Python sections we learned about several variable types, including strings, numbers and Boolean (true or false) variables. Swift is what is known as a 'strongly typed' language, meaning that when a variable is used in a function, that variable has to be of the correct type or the app will crash.

For example, in this code:

```
var number = "2"
var newNumber = number * 5
```

we get an error, because number is defined to be a string, and we cannot multiply strings by integers (whole numbers). To fix that, we can use the Int command to convert number to an integer:

```
var number = "2"
var newNumber = Int(number)! * 5
```

This code now works. Note that we need to put an ! after Int(number) because there is a chance that the conversion will not work. For example, in this code:

```
var number = "test"
var newNumber = Int(number)! * 5
```

we would get a crash, because Swift would not be able to convert the string 'test' to a number.

Finally, if we wanted to multiply a number by a decimal we would need to convert it into a 'float' (ie a 'floating point' number, or a decimal). We would do that using this code:

```
var number = "8.4"
var newNumber = Float(number)! * 5.3
```

Feel free to play with these commands to get to grips with them. In fact, Xcode has a great mode called 'Playgrounds' where you can type in code and see the output straight away, which is perfect for experimentation like this. To create a new playground, click File → New → Playground in Xcode and start typing some code.

Note: If you test out these lines of code in an Xcode playground, you will likely get a warning that 'The variable was never mutated: consider changing var to let'. This is because as well as using var to create a variable in Swift, we can use let to create a constant (ie a variable that doesn't change). This is preferred by Xcode, so if you have a variable that doesn't change value, like number in the above examples, you should define it using let rather than var.

Building an app for iPhone or iPad project: Visitor Registration app

We've now gone on a tour of Xcode and seen how to add labels, buttons and text fields to our app. We've also written some Swift code and created Outlets and Actions to make our app interactive. Finally, we saw some of the intricacies of the Swift language, including optionals and its strongly typed nature.

We're now going to put all this together by building a Visitor Registration app, and of course we're going to set this to you as a challenge. Essentially the app should ask the user for a name and a visit duration in minutes and then convert this duration into an hours and minutes representation. We will then display the result on the screen with a mention of the name entered. Simple. For example, if you enter 'Delphine' and 135 minutes, the app will display a message saying something like 'Thank you for your registration Delphine. See you in 2h 15min (2.25h) for your logout'.

You can notice that the hours and minutes values are integers whereas the duration in hours is a decimal number. Good luck!

Visitor Registration app: solution

Start by creating a new project in Xcode (File→ New → Project) and entering the default settings.

Then create the user interface: drag in a label for the instructions, two text fields, a button, and then a second label for the result. The result should look something like this (8.9):

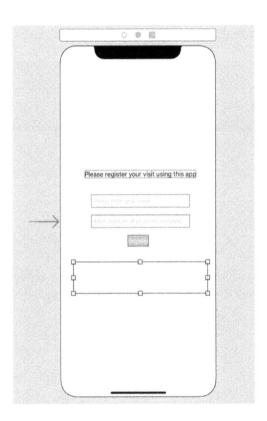

Note the result label is currently blank – we'll add the value with code when the user taps the button.

The next step is to create Outlets for the label and the text fields, and an Action for the button. Do this in the usual way, but ctrl-dragging, until your code looks like this:

```
@IBAction func register(_ sender: Any) {
}
@IBOutlet weak var nameTextField: UITextField!
@IBOutlet weak var durationTextField: UITextField!
@IBOutlet weak var result: UILabel!
```

Finally, we will add the code to the register() method to do the calculation and display the result to the user. First, we get the contents of the text fields (notice that we're using let rather than var as these values will not change):

```
let nameEntered = nameTextField.text!;
let visitDurationEntered = durationTextField.text!
```

Then we convert the visit duration value to an integer – we'll see why just below (don't forget the ! as the result will be an optional):

```
let visitDurationInMinutes = Int(visitDurationEntered)!
```

The duration of the visit in hours, which is a decimal number, is the duration of the visit in minutes divided by 60. To do that, we need to convert the visit duration in minutes to a Float and then do the division:

```
let visitDurationInHours = Float(visitDurationInMinutes)
/ 60
```

We can add a line to round this value, using the round function:

```
let visitDurationInHoursRound = round(100 *
visitDurationInHours) / 100
```

We have the visit duration in hours; the first conversion is done. Now, let's do the conversion to hours and minutes. The hour value is the integer part of the value we get for the duration in hours:

```
let visitDurationHour = Int(visitDurationInHours)
```

Then we can calculate the minutes value, which is an integer, as shown below:

```
let visitDurationMinutes = visitDurationInMinutes -
visitDurationHour * 60
```

That's why visitDurationInMinutes needed to be an integer and not a floating number.

Finally, we update the result label to give the message we need (note we need to convert visitDurationInHoursRound, visitDurationHour and visitDurationMinutes to string here):

```
result.text = "Thank you for your registration " +
nameEntered + ". See you in " + String(visitDurationHour)
+ "h " + String(visitDurationMinutes) + "min (" + String
(visitDurationInHoursRound) + "h) for your logout."
```

Putting it all together, your app should look like this (*8.10*):

8.10

Now run the app, and check that it works. If you've set up everything correctly, you should be able to enter a name and a duration and the app will display a message with the right information (*8.11*):

8.11

Hurrah! All seems to be well, but there is one small problem – if the user doesn't enter a correct duration (a number) into the app, it will crash. Try entering 'two' or any string and you'll see the error. This is because the Int command fails as Swift cannot convert 'two' into a number. To get around this we can use an if statement:

```
if let visitDurationInMinutes = Int(visitDuration
Entered) {
   let visitDurationInHours = Float(visitDurationIn
Minutes) / 60
```

```
    let visitDurationInHoursRound = round(100 *
visitDurationInHours) / 100
    let visitDurationHour = Int(visitDurationInHours)
    let visitDurationMinutes = visitDurationInMinutes -
visitDurationHour * 60
    }
    result.text = "Thank you for your
    registration " + nameEntered + ". See you
    in " + String(visitDurationHour) + "h " +
    String(visitDurationMinutes) + "min (" + String(visit
    DurationInHoursRound) + "h) for your logout."
} else {
    result.text = "Please enter a correct duration."
}
```

This is quite a neat solution – the first line now tests to see if the conversion is possible, and if it is, proceeds to show the result. If it isn't, it displays a friendly error message.

Summary

We've covered a lot of ground in this section. Hopefully you now feel reasonably familiar with Xcode, and you understand the basics of how apps are made. You have seen how the user interface interacts with the code of the app to create a working app which gives the user some information.

Further learning

If you want to double down on learning iOS app development, you can try some of these links:

- www.udemy.com/complete-ios-10-developer-course/ (archived at https://perma.cc/X7GE-E3V6) – Rob's online course in iOS app development.
- www.appcoda.com/ios-programming-course/ (archived at https://perma.cc/E9MQ-SS7E) – free iOS development tutorials.
- https://itunes.apple.com/us/course/developing-ios-8-apps-swift/ id961180099 (archived at https://perma.cc/6B9R-LGG9) – popular Stanford iOS coding course – a little outdated, but good quality and free.
- www.coursera.org/specializations/app-development (archived at https://perma.cc/3FCP-9A7J) – Swift-based iOS development courses.
- www.udacity.com/course/ios-developer-nanodegree--nd003? v=ios1 (archived at https://perma.cc/4MCQ-VPQK) – iOS developer course created by AT&T, Lyft and Google.

## CHAPTER NINE

Windows desktop application programming

W e've looked at programming languages in the previous sections that have enabled us to produce some pretty good results. We've constructed a webpage with HTML, JavaScript and CSS and delivered a basic Python app. But now we're going to delve into something a bit more familiar to a typical workplace, a desktop application. For the purposes of this book, we will build a simple salary enhancement application. This will take a numerical input from the user and apply a percentage increase and display the resultant augmented salary back to the user.

Desktop applications evolution

Desktop applications are extremely useful and powerful tools. Locally deployed, they can harness system resources to run lightning analysis and produce reports, handle real time inputs/outputs from peripheral devices like barcode scanners and RFID tags and connect across company networks to retrieve, query and process large amounts of data. Most likely you already use bespoke software that is particular to your company's line of business. In addition, less pronounced but equally powerful and useful, you use other desktop applications every day – Chrome, Firefox, Edge, WORD, Outlook, Mac Mail. The list is long and familiar.

Over the years there has been a gradual and pronounced shift in the workplace towards more cloud-based solutions – that is, software that runs over the internet and that you typically access via a web browser. However, desktop applications are still very much a primary software solution. They can leverage significant advantages over their cloud-based cousins in terms of performance, security and connectivity (internal business networks tend to be faster and inherently more secure than any access over the internet). Indeed, in most successful companies there is a healthy hybrid of multi-layered solutions involving both cloud-based and desktop lines of business applications.

Microsoft Visual Studio Community Edition

We are going to utilize Microsoft Visual Studio and its inbuilt suite of graphical user interface (GUI) components to produce a first sample application. The beauty of these applications is that they can be easily built and packaged ready for distribution and installation on other devices.

The presentation libraries that we will use for the GUI are Windows-specific and so, if you wish to follow this chapter, then you will need to be running Windows on your PC or Mac.

Specifically, we are going to make use of the Community Edition of Visual Studio. This edition is free to use and all you need is a Microsoft account (Hotmail address, Xbox account or

Office 365 licence for instance). This is an awesome piece of software for a developer and is pretty much a full-feature edition. Perhaps the only thing I've really missed between this and the Enterprise level editions is some of the powerful collaborative features when working in teams of developers.

C# programming language

Within Visual Studio, we are going to make use of the C# programming language. 'Why another language?', I hear you ask. Well, put simply, you can never get enough exposure to different techniques and development tools and what better way to test the water than to dip your toes in as many pools as you can. You are also gaining experience across languages, and one thing you will start to notice is the striking similarity of core concepts between languages. It's not by accident that there is the common convention of conditional if else statements, variables and for loops to name but a few. All of these share a familiar format across the languages we have seen so far – JavaScript, Python and now soon to be C#.

Alongside PHP, C# is a very popular language for developers and is especially prevalent in line of business applications and high-performance scenarios such as gaming (alongside its even more powerful relation C++). Developed and supported by Microsoft, it is a mature and fully featured language choice for a programmer. One aspect I particularly like is the well-struc-tured and consistent nature of the language with fantastic resources online and a very large and active community across the globe. To use an analogy, I might liken PHP and Python to your artisan spoken languages, perhaps Spanish with linguistic variations in Latin and Central American regions, whereas C# is the language of business – universal and functional.

Installation of Visual Studio

Let's get started then, open a browser and using your preferred search engine enter the terms 'Microsoft Visual Studio Community Edition'. Click on the most prominent Microsoft link and you won't go far wrong.

The page should like the below image (*9.1*). If you review the information and features, one of the most striking things, you will learn is that Visual Studio is a very powerful IDE (Integrated Development Environment). It is similar to Brackets which we used in the HTML coding section; however, Visual Studio offers the further ability to code and develop in a multitude of languages, frameworks and platforms including desktop, gaming and mobile app development.

9.1

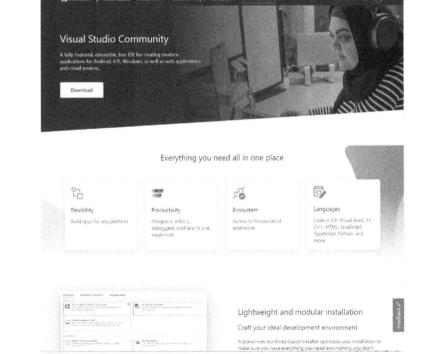

Go ahead and click the Download Community Edition button which is displayed prominently on the page there. This will download an installer .exe file which you can now click to run the Visual Studio Installer. After the obligatory terms and conditions checks and a brief download of components you will be presented with a veritable smorgasbord of development options (9.2).

9.2

You can choose as many as you wish but bear in mind you can always rerun the installer, via this .exe or from within Visual Studio at any point afterwards to add features and environments to your development setup. For now, let's select .NET Desktop Development as per the screenshot image above. You can see that the installer automatically prechecks detailed components on the right-hand side there in conjunction with our selection. We'll leave these as they are currently.

Click Install and then fetch yourself a refreshment as this takes a short while – my installation package was 7.5GB to download and install. The handy installation update screen will keep you informed of the progress (9.3).

9.3

Account sign in

Once you have finished installation, you will need to sign in with a valid Microsoft account (if you haven't got one don't worry– it's quick and simple if you follow the button **Create an account** and, better still, it doesn't cost anything) (9.4).

9.4

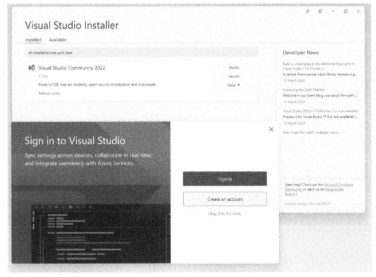

Development settings

When asked, select your desired theme. I am quite partial to light themes but some people much prefer the high contrast of dark backgrounds. It is entirely a personal preference and can be easily switched later from the menu options if you wish to experiment.

You will also be prompted to select desired development settings to tailor the environment. Again, this may be easily changed afterwards, but for now let's go ahead and select Visual C#.

Setting up a new project

From the start page (9.5), select **Create a new project.**

9.5

You'll then be presented with a long list of premade templates to choose from (9.6). For the purposes of this run through we will choose **Windows Forms App (.NET Framework).** You may have to scroll down the list to see this. Be sure to select the C# language version and not the VB language one – this is denoted by the C# tag and the green C# symbol on the icon. Also, be especially careful not to select the similarly named Windows Forms App template. What's the difference and why so similar? Well, basically our selection comes pre-packaged with the .NET framework, which is universally available on any machine running Windows, whereas the other template may require further components to be packaged and installed alongside our application if we were to distribute it.

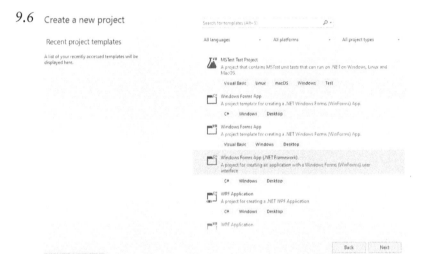

9.6   Create a new project

On the following screen (9.7), give your project a meaningful name. You can leave the other options with their respective preselected values.

The Solution Explorer

We are ready to go! You should now see a development environment with a familiar Windows style form which is in effect our

9.7

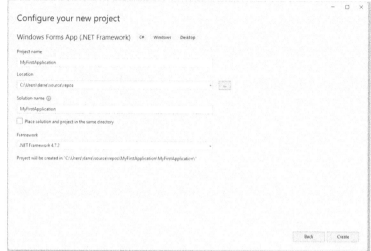

design canvas. Over to the right should be a list of files in the Solution Explorer pane. If you can't see this go to View in the top menu and then, from the dropdown, select Solution Explorer. Your view should look like the image below (9.8):

9.8

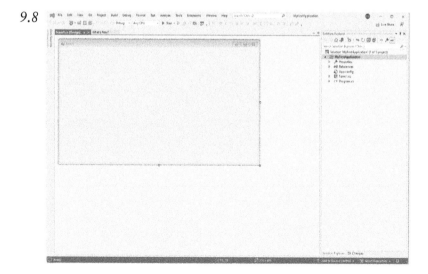

The list of the files on the right-hand side are the files which Visual Studio automatically created for us. We won't worry too much about all the files in this introductory exercise, but the ones we will concentrate on are:

• Form1.cs – this is the code file which contains the information important for displaying our current form and managing its interactivity.
• Program.cs – this is the code file which holds our initial program code and is the entry point for our application. In this example we don't need to worry about this as the template has taken care of it.

NB. We could easily rename these files, particularly important when you start building larger applications with multiple forms and code files, but for now let's leave things simply as they are.

GUI Toolbox magic

To get stuck in, click on [View] from the top menu and then [Toolbox] from the drop-down menu (9.9). You may already have a quick launch tab down the left-hand side of the editor window. This presents a pane which includes a veritable candy store of common user interface components, all neatly categorized for our perusal. Feel free to explore, but then let's settle for the Common Controls category in which you will find familiar controls, e.g. button, text box, etc.

For our application we will need the following components:

• Textbox – for the user to input the salary.
• NumericUpDown – for the user to specify the percentage enhancement to be applied.
• Button – to trigger the calculation when the user is ready.
• Label – to display the result back to the user.

9.9

Go ahead and drag these components from the Toolbox on to our Form in the main window. You may easily adjust their positioning and resize them to achieve a neat and attractive layout. You should now have something which looks similar to the image below (*9.10*).

9.10

Setting properties for our controls

We may change the display and manage the behaviour of each control on our form, and indeed the form itself, through the properties window. From the top menu, select View and then towards the bottom Properties Window. This will display a pane with a range of settings and corresponding values. The settings are linked to the context of the item currently selected on the form. The context may also be the form itself if this is selected. Most likely the form will be the initial context, but now select the various controls to see how the properties window adapts accordingly to display the relevant settings for the selected component. Review the properties and settings for each component; you may need to scroll up and down to see all of them. In fact, there are plenty of expandable sections within the list itself which you may view by clicking the + symbols. When you are ready select the form by clicking anywhere on its frame or blank area.

With the form in selection, scroll to the property [Text] and change its value to 'Salary Enhancer'. Notice how the text at the top of the form, the title of the window, changes to this edited value.

Select the other components in turn, locate the properties and change the values as per the following list:

TEXTBOX
[Name] = txtSalary
[TextAlign] = Right

NUMERIC STEPPER
[Name] = numPercentage
[DecimalPlaces] = 2

BUTTON
[Name] = btnCalculate
[Text] = Calculate

LABEL
[Name] = lblResult
[Text] = Pending Calculation

When you've finished applying changes your form should now look akin to the following screenshot (*9.11*):

9.11

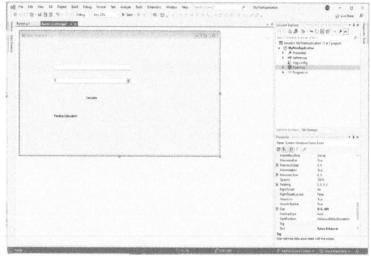

Adding functionality to our application

Each component on our form and the form itself have a variety of events which we can harness and then act on in code. The list of events available is simply huge. Click on the form to place it in selection and then over in the Properties window you'll notice a lightning icon (Events). Click on this and the properties list is replaced with a long list of different events available. As you click on different events Visual Studio gives you a handy explanatory note at the bottom of the Properties window regarding the selected event (*9.12*).

9.12

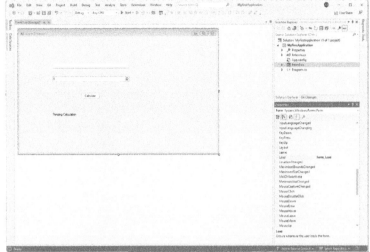

Of particular note is the [Load] event which has a prefilled value of Form_Load. What this means is that, when the form loads, an event is triggered which runs some code in a function called Form_Load. This code function, which we will see shortly, is currently blank and doesn't do anything. It was created automatically for us as a placeholder when we set up the project. For now, select the button component and review its events.

With the button in selection and viewing its events list, scroll down to the event [Click]. It is currently blank meaning that there is no event attached to it (9.13). A button which doesn't do anything is pretty useless, so let's create and bind our own function to this buttons click event. Double-click the blank value box. This will automatically create an event in code ready for us to add our instructions and logic.

The code behind will appear as the tab Form1.cs in the main editor window (don't worry – you can easily flick back to the design editor for your form using the tabs at the top of the window). This view contains the code attached to the form whereas the other tab Form1.cs[Design] is the visual representation or design of the form we have been looking at up until now (9.13).

9.13

What Visual Studio does rather neatly is abstract the code and logic of the form into a different view. This allows you to design and interact with form elements via the graphical editor in a much more user-friendly manner, whilst coding interactivity and business logic in the code view.

Take a closer look at the code. You will see two separate blocks of code called Form_Load and btnCalulate_Click. The start and end of these bocks are denoted by the open and closing curly braces { and }. These blocks of code are called functions and, in this instance, are executed when our events fire. Recall that Form_Load was the entry in the Forms Load event setting that was automatically created for us. btnCalulate_Click was created for us when we double clicked the Click event entry for our button component. Notice how Visual Studio took the name of our component and appended _Click to it. It was important for us to rename all our components at the start, because once we start developing complex forms with lots of elements and events it is important to be able to identify each easily.

Don't worry too much about the rest of the syntax and other elements in this code file. It is beyond the scope of this introduction to go into detail, but feel free to read up. However, a very quick indication is as follows.

The **using statements** at the top basically import a bunch of libraries which instantiate and enable our form and components. They also open up a massive amount of pre-built functionality to us for use in our own code.

Private and public are scope access modifiers and govern where the relevant functions may be called from. In large applications with multiple forms, you don't inadvertently want some code on one form calling the code from another which just so happens to have an identically named function.

The special function **public Form** is called a constructor and runs when our form is first created. You can see it calls another function called InitializeComponent() which is a system function responsible for creating our form and hooking up all the code at runtime.

The items next to the function names in brackets are called parameters. They are essentially bits of information which are passed into the function when it is called. This will include a reference to the component which was clicked (our button) and other information which may be relevant to the context.

Coding our button click

Phew! Well, we've covered a lot rather quickly, let's write some code.

C# is a little different from Python programming which we looked at in Chapter 6. Whilst it also uses variables, C# is a strongly typed language. This means that you must denote the type of data that your variable will contain ahead of assigning it. The advantage of this rigidity is improved performance and robustness.

Principal data types in C# are:

char – individual characters
string – for text

int – for whole numbers

double, float, decimal– for real numbers with decimal places (the types have different levels of precision / numbers after the decimal point).

boolean – true or false

datetime – dates and time

The syntax for declaring a variable is much the same as Python. However, you must remember to specify the data type first e.g.

[data type] [variable name] = [value];

e.g.

string myName = "Darren";
int myAge = 45;

Important – note the semi-colon ; at the end of the statement. Each declarative statement in C# must end with a ; . Additionally, whereas Python uses indentation to separate parts of code, C# uses open and closing curly braces to denote blocks of code and functionality (we have already seen this when we look at the functions of our button and form in the code file).

In addition to variables that we might create, we can also access the form elements and their properties directly, which is essential when coding interactivity into our application and working with our form. Let's do this now.

In the Form1.cs code view, locate the function btnCalculate_ Click and write some new code in between the curly braces:

```
private void btnCalculate_Click(object sender,
EventArgs e)
{
decimal salary = txtSalary.Text;
}
```

This code declares a variable called salary, data types it as a decimal and then assigns the value entered into our text box on our form to it. We access the value of the text box from its [Text] property.

Did you notice that as you typed Visual Studio's IntelliSense was popping up smart suggestions? Once you'd typed txtSalary to reference the text box on our form, the dot suddenly made all the properties and events available in the IntelliSense list. This is Visual Studio actively helping and predicting the information and code we might be writing. It is an incredibly powerful and smart feature and will invariably ensure your efficiency as a programmer.

But something is wrong: txtSalary.Text is highlighted with a squiggly underscore. If you hover over the text IntelliSense appears with an explanation of the error and suggestions for fixing it:

Cannot implicitly convert string to decimal

What Visual Studio is highlighting to us here is that we have declared our variable salary as a data type decimal, and we are trying to assign the value from the text box which will be of a type string by default. The solution is simply to use C#'s inbuilt functionality to convert the text into a number before assigning it.

```
private void btnCalculate_Click(object sender,
EventArgs e)
{
        decimal salary = Convert.ToDecimal(txtSalary.
        Text);
}
```

Now that we have the value entered into the text box stored in our variable it is time to capture the salary percentage increase from the numeric stepper control and apply the enhancement.

```
private void btnCalculate_Click(object sender,
EventArgs e)
{
        decimal salary = Convert.ToDecimal(txtSalary.
        Text);
decimal enhanced_salary = salary * (1 + numPercentage.
Value/100);
}
```

Examining the new line of code, we are declaring a new variable to store our augmented salary. We are then assigning this the value of our variable salary multiplied by the Value property of our numeric stepper component which we called numPercentage. Note that, in this case we don't need to convert the value of the numeric stepper as it is already held as a decimal data type.

Lastly, to finish off our form we need to output the result of our calculation to the label on our form.

```
private void btnCalculate_Click(object sender,
EventArgs e)
{
        decimal salary = Convert.ToDecimal(txtSalary.
        Text);

        decimal enhanced_salary = salary * (1 +
        numPercentage.Value/100);
lblResult.Text = enhanced_salary.ToString();
}
```

We set the Text property of our label component (which we named lblResult) to the value of our variable enhanced_salary. We need to convert it to a string as the label component expects a string for its Text property. Note that we could have written Convert.ToString(enhanced_salary); however the Tostring() is a shortened alternative and clearer to read.

Running our application

We've coded our application; our button click is in place and our user interaction is ready to be tested, so it is time to run it.

In the top menu bar, you will see a prominent green arrow and the label [Start]. Click on this and Visual Studio will fire up our application (*9.14*).

9.14

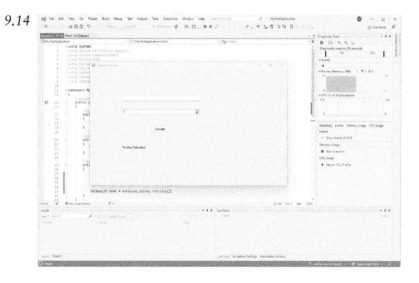

Visual Studio is running our application and allowing us to interact with it exactly as if it were a deployed application. Visual Studio is operating it in a debug mode; you can observe the diagnostic and metrics panes which have appeared in the IDE window. Additionally, any code errors which occur will jump back to the editor and highlight the precise line and nature of the error. It is important to test software prior to release and the debug features and tools available to you as a developer using Visual Studio are extensive and top class.

With our application running perform the following actions:

Enter the value 25000 in the text box.
Select 15 from on the numeric stepper.
Click the Calculate button.

The output 28750.00 should be displayed (*9.15*).

9.15

If else conditional statements

Recall that we studied if else statements in the earlier Python chapter. C# uses if else statements in the same way, just with slightly different syntax. Let's use if else to adjust our code to validate the user has selected a percentage increment.

```
private void btnCalculate_Click(object sender,
EventArgs e)
{
        decimal salary = Convert.ToDecimal(txtSalary.
        Text);
decimal enhanced_salary;
if(numPercentage.Value > 0)
{
        enhanced_salary = salary * (1 + numPercentage.
        Value/100);
lblResult.Text = enhanced_salary.ToString();
}else{
        lblResult.Text = "Please enter a value for the
        increase";
}
}
```

We have introduced an if condition which checks to see whether or not the user has inputted a value into the numeric stepper i.e. > 0. Notice that we now declare the variable enhanced_salary but we don't assign any value to it until later in the code within the if statement.

Just like in the Python examples we have previously studied, we control the flow of the program based on a conditional check. The only difference here is that instead of indentation for the different code paths, here we use open and close curly braces for the relevant block of code.

If the entered value is greater than 0, we execute our salary enhancement code in the first code block demarked by the first open and close curly braces:

```
enhanced_salary = salary * (1 + numPercentage.
Value/100);

lblResult.Text = enhanced_salary.ToString();
```

If not, we drop down to the else code block and execute the line of code between its open and closing curly braces:

```
lblResult.Text = "Please enter a value for the
increase";
```

Building your application

We are now ready to build our application. From the top menu, select [Build] and then from the drop down click [Build Solution]. You should now see a progress indicator followed shortly by a Build succeeded message on the left of the bottom blue ribbon at the base of the Visual Studio window. Conversely if there are errors, Visual Studio will not allow the build to succeed and will be quite verbose in highlighting these to you with explanations in the output window.

Navigate to your project's build location – by default on Windows this is:

C:\Users\[user]\source\repos\MyFirstApplication

You may have named your project differently of course so switch out MyFirstApplication accordingly and also your Windows username for [User].

If you are still unsure of an application's location, you can always go to the [Solution Explorer] pane and right click on the solution (the top item in the list). Then in the [Properties] window you will see the entry [Path] and the value which will be the directory location of your project.

Click down into the sub directory MyFirstApplication and locate the bin folder. Within there you will find Debug and Release folders. Look in the Debug folder and therein will be an .exe (executable) file. You can launch this .exe directly by double clicking on it and your fabulous Windows application will run as an independent program.

You can share this .exe file on any modern Windows machine and it will run your application as you see it now (subject to permissions). The image below shows my application .exe running on a separate machine in my office launched on a double click (*9.16*).

9.16

Optimizing for release

A last step before deploying your application would be to configure and optimize for release. To do so, go back to Visual Studio and from the same top menu item [Build] this time chose the very last item on the drop down [Configuration Manager]. From the window that pops ups, change the top selection in the drop down from Debug to Release. Now build the solution as before. This time the .exe will be deposited in the Release sub directory instead of the Debug one. In the background Visual Studio has optimized the application and removed all the debugging features and associated overhead from the outputted .exe file.

Congratulations on successfully writing your first software application! We have obviously barely scratched the surface, but hopefully this introduction has given you the confidence for further exploration and research. Furthermore, we hope it inspires you to build more sophisticated and fully featured applications.

## CHAPTER TEN

Building an app for Android

With over 85 per cent of the smartphone market (as of 2016), Android is by far the biggest mobile platform. It is also the one that requires the least investment, as apps can be built using Windows, Mac or Linux. In this chapter we'll go through the process of creating a simple Android app, much in the same way we did with the iPhone app in the previous chapter.

While iOS development uses Apple's own language, Swift, Android development uses Java (a very different language to JavaScript, used primarily in web development). Java is a great language to learn as it is used in a huge range of platforms, including web apps, Windows and Mac programs, scientific applications and Internet Of Things devices.

We will start by downloading Android Studio, which is the equivalent of Xcode for Android development. It is built by Google, is completely free, and is the only software you need to make Android apps. It's not quite as user-friendly as Xcode, and can be quite slow, but it is also more flexible, and has features such as Instant Run, which allow you to test run your apps on the simulator without recompiling them.

Once we've downloaded Android Studio, we'll take a tour of the interface and run a Hello World app. Then we'll add labels and buttons, build in some interactivity and finally make a simple app that prompts us with a reminder for a performance review.

Without further ado then, let's get started.

Downloading and setting up Android studio

The main Android developer site is at developer.android.com – it is well worth clicking through and reading some of the introductory guides to learn about Android features and style guides for developers. Once you've done that, you can download Android Studio at developer.android.com/studio.

On that page click the big green download button, agree to the terms and conditions and you're good to go. It installs like any other piece of software, and since Android Studio 2.2 you no longer need to download Java separately (which makes life much easier!).

Once you have installed Android Studio, run it and you'll likely be prompted to install various updates. Our advice would be to choose all the default options, keep pressing Next and let the software do its thing. After a few minutes you should see the Welcome to Android Studio screen.

Click 'Start a new Android Studio project' and you'll see the Choose Your Project screen.

You'll see the different Form Factors displayed as tabs across the top showing the different devices your app will support. The default is phone and tablet. We are only covering phone and tablet in this introduction, so we'll stick with the default for now.

In the section immediately below, you'll see a range of activity icons, which allows you to choose a default activity. An activity in Android development is a single screen within our app. It is like a page on a website, so within a single app we might have a login activity, an activity which shows a list of users and perhaps a settings activity.

Here we have several activity templates that we can choose from, which are useful in a number of cases, but we'll start with the simplest (and default) – the Empty Activity.

The next screen allows us to configure our project.

- The application name can be anything you like – try something like My First App.
- The package name is similar to a normal domain name, such as google.com, but you don't have to actually own the domain name. So, you could use rob.percival.com, or yourcompany-name.com. It doesn't matter what you use now, but if you submit your app to Google Play, the package name will become part of the unique package ID for your app, so you might want to use something that represents your name or your company name.
- You can change the project location if you wish or leave it as the default – this is where the project files will be stored.
- For the code language we are going to choose Java from the dropdown.

You'll notice that you can choose the oldest version of Android you would like to support. The older the version you choose, the more devices you will be able to support; but you will lose access to some of the latest features.

Our advice would be to choose the default version (in our case Ice Cream Sandwich) – this usually provides a good balance of modern features and large device support.

When you are ready, click Finish and our app development environment will be set up.

And you're done. After a few seconds to create your app, you should see the main Android Studio interface.

It doesn't look particularly friendly, but we can break it down into three main parts:

- The top bar has the usual save, open, copy, paste menu options, as well as the green 'play' triangle which you will use to run your app.
- The left pane shows the file structure within your app.
- The main window shows the contents of the file we are currently editing, in this case the MainActivity Java file.

The other buttons and menus we can ignore for now – we'll use some of them later but most you will only need if you're doing some advanced Android app development.

That's the setup complete. Before we start customizing our app we'll quickly run through the process of running an app on an Android Virtual Device (AVD).

Running your first Android app

Running your app is simple – in a moment you will just press the green 'play' button in the top menu bar.

But first we need to create a Virtual Device. Adjacent to the green arrow there is a drop down, initially with the text No Devices because we haven't set up any Virtual Devices yet. Drop this down and click on Open AVD Manager. This is where all your Virtual Devices are managed. Click on + Create Virtual Device. You can now choose from a selection of different phones and tablets. You can choose whichever one you like – we will stick with the default, the Pixel 2.

Next, you can choose to install any version of Android on your Virtual Device.

Unless you particularly want a specific version, we would recommend using the default, in our case Q. Selecting this will download and install the relevant development and framework files.

Finally, you can give your device a name, and choose some advanced options, such as whether the device starts in portrait or landscape orientation. We would recommend keeping to the default options for now.

Congratulations, you're done! Select that device, click Run and the device will start up and eventually (after around 2–5 minutes depending on your machine) display your app in the Android Emulator.

You've run your first Android app but, of course, it doesn't do much yet, so let's see how to customize the UI (user interface) of our app.

Adding text and buttons

We'll be writing some Java shortly, but first let's see how to add text and buttons to our apps. Just above the main editing window, you should see two tabs: activity_main.xml and MainActivity. java.

Click the activity_main.xml tab and you should see a screen showing the layout of the app. Click on the Hello World text and you see something like this (10.1):

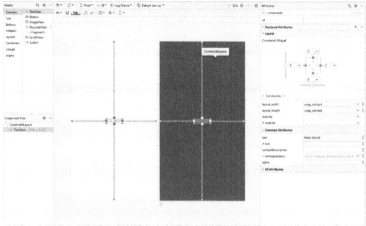

This window is divided into four main areas:

- The Palette in the top left has a long list of elements that you can add to your app, such as Buttons, CheckBoxes and Switches.
- The Component Tree in the bottom left shows all the elements that have already been added to your app, and how they are related to each other (in our case, we have a single TextView, which is inside the activity_main layout).
- The main editing window shows a preview of your app, and allows you to drag elements around the screen.
- The Properties window shows the properties of the currently selected element (in this case the Hello World text).

Spend a few minutes experimenting with adding different widgets to the screen, changing their properties and moving them around.

Challenge 1

Try to recreate this layout (*10.2*):

10.2

Solution:

Firstly, take the 'Hello World' textView and drag it into the centre of the screen – you should see a blue layout guide appear to show you that it is correctly centred. Over in the right-hand panes, you can also view the constraint widget under the layout section, to assist you in centring the element. In the Properties window change the 'text' field from 'Hello World' to 'My Great App'. Then, in the textAppearance drop-down menu, select Large. Your text label should now display as in the picture above. You may be viewing both the Design and Blueprint views at the same time. You can select just the Design view from the drop down, which can be found in the top left corner of the design pane (layered square panes icon).

To add the button, find Button in the Palette and drag it on to the screen, centred and slightly underneath the textView. Change the text to 'Click Me!' in the 'text' field of the button Properties. To correctly position elements, you may need to play around with the horizontal and vertical bias sliders in the Constraint Widget under Layout in the right-hand pane.

That's it. Feel free to experiment further with changing colours, trying different layouts etc. If an option isn't visible in the Properties window, click the View All Properties link to view all the available options. You can customize pretty much anything there.

Making the app interactive

If you run the app again (it should be much quicker this time!) you'll see the layout appear on the Virtual Device screen, but if you click the button, you'll notice that nothing happens. Just like with iOS development, we need to write some code to make the button do something, but the process is a little different.

Before we write any code, with Android development we need to set the 'onClick' property for the button to tell the app the name of the 'method' that we want to run when the button is clicked. A method is essentially the same as a function – a chunk of code that we can run by referring to its name.

To set this up, click on the button and type 'buttonClicked' in the onClick field. Now we need to write the buttonClicked method.

We do this in the MainActivity.java file, so click on the MainActivity.java tab above the editing window. In that file you'll see the following code:

```
package com.example.robpercival.myfirstapp;

import android.support.v7.app.AppCompatActivity;
import android.os.Bundle;

public class MainActivity extends AppCompatActivity {
```

```
@Override
protected void onCreate(Bundle savedInstanceState) {
super.onCreate(savedInstanceState);
setContentView(R.layout.activity_main);
}
}
```

This is Java, and we'll run through it line by line. Don't aim for a complete understanding of every aspect of the code at this point – that will come later. For now, just make sure you have a fair overview of what each part of the code is doing. You can always Google particular keywords if you would like more information.

The first line defines the name of the package, or app – in our case:

```
com.example.robpercival.myfirstapp.
```

The 'import' lines bring in various 'libraries', which allow you to work with specific features, such as textViews, buttons, log files or even GPS. These two default lines give us the default code required to run our activity and use the Android OS (operating system).

Next, we're creating a 'class' called MainActivity. A class is a collection of methods (chunks of code that serve a particular function) and variables. This particular class will control the Main Activity. As we only have one activity in our app, this class essentially controls our whole app.

The class is 'public', which means it can be accessed from anywhere in the app (and, potentially, by other apps as well). It 'extends' the AppCompatActivity class, which is a default class that contains a collection of methods that we can use with our activity.

Next, we build a method called onCreate. This method is a default one, which is run when the activity is 'created', ie when the app is run. This is a 'protected' method, meaning that it can be accessed from anywhere in the app, but not by other apps.

The 'void' in this line means that the method doesn't return anything. To understand what this means, imagine a method called 'plus' which adds two numbers together. For that method to work, you would need to pass two numbers to the method, and then it would return the total of those two numbers. The onCreate method runs some code, but doesn't return anything, which is confirmed by the 'void' in the method definition.

The super.onCreate(savedInstanceState); line runs all the default code needed when the app is run. The savedInstanceState contains the previous state of the app, and in some circumstances can be used to return the app to that state (for example, returning the user to an email that they were previously writing in the app).

Finally, setContentView(R.layout.activity_main); establishes that we want to use activity_main to define our layout, or ContentView. This will display the user interface layout that we have created.

Phew! There is a lot of theory there, and don't worry at this point if not everything is completely clear – it will make much more sense as you start to build more apps. For now a broad understanding is all that is needed.

Writing the code for the button

Just underneath the 'public class MainActivity…' line, write the following code:

```
public void buttonClicked(View view) {

}
```

This creates a public method ('public') which doesn't return anything ('void') called buttonClicked. This method will be run when our button is clicked. The curly braces ({ and }) contain the code for our method.

The 'View view' part is a little more complicated, so read carefully. Firstly, a 'view' is anything that appears on the screen (so buttons, textViews etc are all 'views').

Secondly, to create a variable in Java, we start with the variable type, and then use the name that we want the variable to be called. So if we want to create a string called 'name' we would type:

```
String name;
```

If we wanted to create an integer called 'number' we would type

```
int number;
```

Here we are creating a variable called 'view' which is of a type View. We need this because when the button is clicked, it runs the buttonClicked method, and it sends some information about itself to that method. That information is stored in this variable 'view', which is of a type of View.

You might want to read that last paragraph a couple of times. Hopefully that makes sense, but if not don't worry, it will become clearer as we carry on.

When you have finished writing the code, you will see a blue callout pointing to the word View (*10.3*):

10.3

```
blic class Main    android.view.View?       :Ac
   public void buttonClicked(View view) {
         |
   }
```

277

This is because to use the variable type View we need to add the View class to our app. To do that, press alt-enter when the blue callout is shown. The callout will then disappear and View will turn black (*10.4*):

10.4

```
public void buttonClicked(View view) {
```

If you click the small '+' next to 'import ...' near the top of the code window, you will see that we now have the View class added to our project:

```
import android.support.v7.app.AppCompatActivity;
import android.os.Bundle;
import android.view.View;
```

If you are having difficulty with the alt+enter shortcut you can just type the import statement in directly.

Making a toast

OK. We have now created the method that will run when the button is clicked. Don't worry – we're nearly done. We now just need to write some code inside that method. We're going to create what is known as a 'toast' – a small piece of text that will display at the bottom of the phone screen for a small period of time. (It is called a 'toast' because it pops up like toast from a toaster.)

To do that, add the following code to the buttonClicked method:

```
Toast.makeText(this, "Hi there!", Toast.LENGTH_SHORT).
show();
```

Hint: when you start typing 'Toast', you will see a drop-down like this (*10.5*):

10.5

Press Enter when Create a new Toast is selected, and it will auto-fill most of the code for you. Nice!

This code creates a new toast with the text 'Hi there!' LENGTH_SHORT refers to the amount of time the toast stays on the screen (you can change it to LENGTH_LONG if you want the toast to stay there longer).

Note: What is 'this'? The 'this' in the toast command refers to the activity that we are currently in, ie MainActivity. This is the context that the toast will appear in.

We're finally done. Your finished code should look like this:

```
package com.example.robpercival.myfirstapp;
import android.support.v7.app.AppCompatActivity;
import android.os.Bundle;
import android.view.View;
import android.widget.Toast;
public class MainActivity extends AppCompatActivity {
public void buttonClicked(View view) {
Toast.makeText(this, "Hi there!", Toast.LENGTH_SHORT).
    show();
}
@Override
    protected void onCreate(Bundle savedInstanceState)
{
```

```
        super.onCreate(savedInstanceState);
        setContentView(R.layout.activity_main);
    }
}
```

Now run the app, and click the button. If you've done everything correctly, you will see the 'Hi there!' message appear at the bottom of the screen like this (10.6):

10.6

Congratulations! That wasn't easy but what we have done is quite advanced – we have created a method called 'button-Clicked' and linked that method to the button that we added to the user interface. Then we added code to that method to display the 'Hi there' text as a toast on the user's screen. Not bad!

Allowing the user to enter some text

So far, all our interactivity goes one way. We don't have any way to get any information from the user, so let's add that functionality to our app.

In Android Studio, go back to the activity_main.xml tab, and in the Palette scroll down until you see Text Fields. There are a number of different types of text field that we can add, which are used for specific data-types. So if you use the 'Phone' type, for example, a specific keyboard will appear to make it easier for the user to enter a phone number. For now, we will just use the Plain Text text field.

Note: a text field in Android development is called an EditText. We will use that in our Java code later on.

Drag the button downwards on the phone screen layout to make space for the text field, and then drag in a Plain Text text field, so your layout looks like this (*10.7*):

10.7
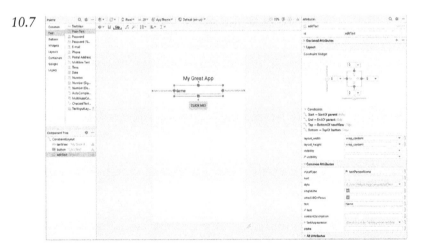

Click on the text field and you'll see a set of properties and drop-downs. Note that there are two sections: Common Attributes which, as the name suggests, contains commonly used attributes; and the All Attributes section containing everything:

- ID
- Layout_width
- Layout_height
- inputType
- hint
- style
- singleline
- selectAllOnFocus
- text
- contentDescription
- textAppearance

The two particularly useful fields here are 'hint' and 'text'. 'text' gives a default value to display in the text field, and 'hint' gives an instruction to the user, such as 'Enter your email address'.

We are going to use this text field to get the user's name, so remove Name from the text field and enter 'What is your name?' into the hint field.

When you run the app, you'll see this layout (*10.8*):

10.8

If you tap on the 'What is your name?' text view, you will be able to enter your name (the hint disappears when you start typing).

We're nearly ready to write some code. We will need to be able to refer to this text view in our code, so we need to know its ID. In the properties, you'll see it has the default ID of editText. You can change this to anything you like – in this case you could use something like nameEditText.

Accessing the entered text

Now all that remains is to get the value of the text that the user has entered in our code. Our aim here is to change the content of the toast so that instead of saying 'Hi there!' it says 'Hi Rob' (if the user has entered Rob as their name, of course).

So, click on the MainActivity.java tab, and enter the following code just above the toast command:

```
EditText nameEditText = (EditText) findViewById(R.
id.nameEditText);
```

You will again receive the blue prompt, this time regarding the EditText widget. Simply press alt+enter when the blue prompt is showing. This will automatically add the relevant import android. widget.EditText; statement at the top of the code. There's quite a lot going on here. First, we're creating a variable of a type EditText called nameEditText. We will use this to refer to our text view.

Ignoring the (EditText) for a moment, the findViewById method finds a view by its ID, and we give it the ID of our text view, which is stored in Resources ('R').

What about that strange (EditText)? Remember that everything that appears on the screen is a 'view'. This applies to text views (EditTexts) as well. The findViewById method returns a generic view, but we know that it is really an EditText, so we use (EditText) to 'cast', or convert, the view into an EditText. Makes sense? You might want to read that paragraph again just to be sure.

Now we have a variable we can use to refer to our text view. The next step is to get the value of the text view, which we'll store in a string called 'name':

```
String name = nameEditText.getText().toString();
```

The String name part creates a string variable called 'name', and then we use getText() to get the text the user entered into the text field, and finally we use toString() to convert it to a string. So far so good!

Finally, we need to change the code for the toast to say hi to our user:

```
Toast.makeText(this, "Hi " + name, Toast.LENGTH_SHORT).
show();
```

Here we have changed 'Hi there' to 'Hi' + name. The '+' combines the two strings, so if the user enters 'Helen' as their name, 'Hi' + name. will be equal to 'Hi Helen'.

That's it. Your code should now look like this:

```
package com.example.robpercival.myfirstapp;

import android.support.v7.app.AppCompatActivity;
import android.os.Bundle;
import android.view.View;
import android.widget.EditText;
import android.widget.Toast;

public class MainActivity extends AppCompatActivity {

public void buttonClicked(View view) {

  EditText nameEditText = (EditText) findViewById
  (R.id.nameEditText);

  String name = nameEditText.getText().toString();

Toast.makeText(this, "Hi " + name, Toast.LENGTH_SHORT).
show();
}

  @Override
  protected void onCreate(Bundle savedInstanceState) {
    super.onCreate(savedInstanceState);
    setContentView(R.layout.activity_main);
  }
}
```

Run the app, enter your name and click the button. If everything has gone well you should see something like this (*10.9*):

10.9

Well done! You now have an app which can collect some data from the user, process it and display it back to the user as a toast. This is the fundamental basis for all user interaction within apps. Give yourself a pat on the back!

Building an app for Android project: performance review reminder app

Now it's time for you to put everything you have learnt into action. As a rough school of thought, successful entrepreneurs have about three great business ideas a year. Why not aim for the top level?! We are going to use this ratio to allow the user to enter their age, and then display back to them the number of good ideas they should have clocked up in toast. Hopefully this will provide some inspiration to get entrepreneuring!

As with the app in the iOS chapter, you will need to convert the user's entered data from a string into an integer, and then multiply it by three, and then convert it back to a string to display the new value to the user. We're going to leave that to you to figure out (using Google is very much allowed, and positively encouraged).

That's it – start from scratch and create a new project. Good luck!

Solution

The setup process for the app is very similar to the previous app – choose all the same options except the app title, which can be anything you like. We called ours Great Ideas.

Once the app is ready, start by creating the user interface. We have used a very similar layout to our previous app.

We have changed the text of the TextView to 'Your Age', and changed the 'hint' of the EditText to 'How old are you?' We've also changed the type of the EditText to 'number' – bonus points if you did that. We changed the EditText's ID to ageEditText.

Next, we changed the button text to 'Show Number of Ideas' and used an onClick method name of showNumberIdeas, which is a little more descriptive than 'buttonClicked' as we used before.

Now over to the code itself. In MainActivity.java, we started by creating the method showNumberIdeas which will be run when the button is clicked:

```
public void showNumberIdeas(View view) {
}
```

Next, we added a line to create a variable called ageEditText to refer to our text field:

```
EditText ageEditText = (EditText) findViewById(R.
id.ageEditText);
```

Next we needed to get the value of the field, convert it to an integer, multiply it by 7 and then convert it back to a string. You likely needed to do some googling to figure out how to do this part – if you managed it, congratulations!

```
String age = ageEditText.getText().toString();
int ageInt = Integer.parseInt(age);
int ideasInt = ageInt * 3;
String numberIdeasString = Integer.toString (ideasInt);
```

Hopefully it's fairly clear what is going on. The first line gets the value entered into ageEditText, the next line converts it to an integer using the method Integer.parseInt. The next line creates a new integer, ideasInt, which is equal to the previous value multiplied by 3. The final line converts this back to a string using the method Integer.toString.

Finally, we used a toast command to display the number of ideas to the user:

```
Toast.makeText(this, "You should have come up with"
+ numberIdeasString + "ideas by now", Toast.LENGTH_
SHORT).show();
```

This time we use two '+'s, as we have some text both before and after the catAgeString.

That's it. Your final complete code should look like this:

```
package com.example.myapplication;

import androidx.appcompat.app.AppCompatActivity;
import android.os.Bundle;
import android.view.View;
import android.widget.EditText;
import android.widget.Toast;

public class MainActivity extends AppCompatActivity {

  public void showNumberIdeas(View view) {
      EditText ageEditText = (EditText) findViewById(R.
      id.ageEditText);
      String age = ageEditText.getText().toString();
      int ageInt = Integer.parseInt(age);
      int numberIdeasInt = ageInt * 3;

      String numberIdeasString = Integer.toString(number
      IdeasInt);

      Toast.makeText(this, "You should have come up with"
      + numberIdeasString + "ideas by now!",
Toast.LENGTH_SHORT).show();
      }

      @Override
      protected void onCreate(Bundle savedInstanceState) {
      super.onCreate(savedInstanceState);
      setContentView(R.layout.activity_main);
   }
}
```

When you run the app and enter an age you should see the result pop up!

Summary

Congratulations! You've built your first complete Android app, and are well on the way to building any app you want. As with most app development, the most difficult hurdle is getting started, which you have already overcome. Well done!

If you want to get further into app development, the single best thing you can do is to pick an app idea and make it. It doesn't have to be a world-beating idea, a simple app like a to-do list app or an egg timer would be fine for your first app. Every time you need to do something you haven't done before, just search the web for what it is you're trying to do and you'll likely find someone who has struggled before you, and someone else who has given them the answer (usually on stackoverflow.com).

If you would like a more structured course to follow to master Android development, go to www.udemy.com/complete-android-n-developer-course/ to check out Rob's Android Developer Course.

Now that you have learned the basics of web, iOS and Android development, we are going to dive into an all-important topic: debugging. Bugs are something that you'll come up against constantly when you're building a website or app (and usually after you've 'finished' it as well). We'll look at some methods of squashing bugs, working out what is causing the problem, searching the web for answers and posting questions online if you can't find a solution.

For now though, give yourself a pat on the back, have a cup of tea and a break, and take a moment to dream of all those great Android apps you could build.

Further learning

Here are a few larger courses if you want to learn Android app development in more detail:

- www.udemy.com/complete-android-n-developer-course/ (archived at https://perma.cc/3GGJ-TKZH) – Rob's online Android course, covering all aspects of Android development.
- https://developer.android.com/training/basics/firstapp/index. html (archived at https://perma.cc/S86H-UV9Q) – official Google training materials in Android development.
- www.coursera.org/specializations/android-app-development (archived at https://perma.cc/52G9-LHTG) – range of beginner and advanced Android courses.
- www.udacity.com/course/developing-android-apps--ud853 (archived at https://perma.cc/3GGJ-TKZH) – free Android course, created by Google.

CHAPTER ELEVEN

Debugging

If you're reading this far in, you should now have some experience in coding in a range of different platforms and languages. Within web development, you've coded in HTML, CSS and JavaScript, using a text editor and a browser to run your code. You've coded in Python using the online compiler at https://repl. it/languages/python. You've also built an iPhone app using Swift and Xcode (if you have access to a Mac) and an Android app using Java and Android Studio.

One thing you'll likely have come across on all of these platforms, and in all of these languages, is bugs. A bug occurs when any piece of code doesn't run as intended. They vary considerably in severity, from a bug which stops your code running at all (such as forgetting the semicolon at the end of a line in Java), to a CSS issue which causes your website logo to display a little lower down than you'd like it.

In this section we'll start by considering why you might want to learn debugging even if you are not planning to take your coding career any further. Next we'll look at some standard debugging processes (and how you can apply some of them to non-coding related problems in your work or life in general). Finally, we'll look at some specific debugging tools and techniques for the platforms that we've covered so far: web (HTML, CSS and JavaScript), iOS (Swift and Xcode) and Android (Java and Android Studio).

Why learn debugging?

Debugging is not just about fixing errors, it's about making your code better. And this has applications in all aspects of life. If your job involves teaching, learning how the recipients of your knowledge find your style is crucial to improving. If you do a lot of number crunching, a small tweak in your Excel formulas could speed up the whole process dramatically (or make you less likely to make a mistake).

What is particularly useful about debugging is that the exact same techniques can be applied to almost anything you do in life, to make you more effective and efficient. Once you start looking at your code, working out where it is going wrong and fixing it, you won't be able to help applying similar techniques to your life as a whole. It's like a coding-based self-improvement program!

Why do I spend so much time debugging?

One question that plagues new coders is why they spend so much time fixing problems in their code. Most people hope that because they have a clear idea in their head about how their code should work, that will automatically transfer itself to your computer screen and everything will run as intended.

The reality is rather different. As you write more and more code, you'll realize that debugging is actually a major part of the app- or website-building process, and this is fine. Computers are fickle beasts, and us mere mortals are not used to interacting with machines that require absolute precision, and will punish you relentlessly by running your code *exactly as you wrote it.*

So debugging is a (big) part of the process. But that doesn't mean that isn't frustrating and we shouldn't try to avoid it as much as possible. So let's start by seeing how we can write code that requires minimal debugging.

How to write code that requires minimal debugging

Step 0: Write good code

Good, clean code can save a huge amount of time in the long run. When you want to build an app or add a new feature to your website, the temptation is often to write your code as quickly as possible and to have the attitude that, as long as it works, it is good enough. This approach is perfectly reasonable when you're learning or for small personal projects, but in our experience it almost always costs you more time than it saves you. Taking an extra five minutes properly writing your code in the first place can save you hours of debugging further down the line.

Compare these two JavaScript functions, which determine whether a number is prime or not. (A *prime number* has precisely two factors, 1 and itself. For example, 2, 3, 5, 7, 11 etc.)

```
function isPrime(x) {
        for ( var i = 2; i < num; i++ )
        { if ( x % i == 0 )
        { return false; } } return true;

}

function isPrime(numberToCheck) {
```

```
// Loop through all numbers less than numberToCheck
    for ( var divisor = 2; divisor < numberToCheck;
    divisor++ ) {
    if ( numberToCheck % divisor == 0 ) {
    // If divisor divides numberToCheck exactly,
        numberToCheck is not prime, so return false
    return false;
    }
    }
// If we get here, we have checked all numbers from 2
up to numberToCheck, and none of them divide into it,
so numberToCheck must be prime
        return true;
}
```

Both functions work perfectly well (the logic is identical for both), but the second function has numerous advantages over the first:

- It is well spaced out. Most programming languages don't require line breaks, but including them makes the code much easier to read.
- It has meaningful variable names. Try to avoid using variable names such as 'x' or 'number', and instead give your variables easy to recognize names.
- It has comments. All programming languages have a way to add human-readable comments, and you should use them whenever possible to explain what your code is doing.

You might feel that in an example like this it doesn't make too much difference whether you use comments, spacing and meaningful variable names, but when your code starts to expand to hundreds of lines (which it will if you are building cool things!), you'll appreciate getting into this habit with all code you write.

Another advantage of coding this way is that it forces you to slow down, making it much less likely that you will miss a crucial semicolon, or miss-spell a function name.

One other trick as you are writing your code is to check it as regularly as possible. This means running your app, or loading your website, and making sure it is behaving as expected so far. As a general guide, if you haven't checked code that you have been writing for over 10 minutes, it might be time to start to get a little nervous and look for a good place to stop and check that everything is OK.

The precise timings will depend on the project and your personality, but our advice, particularly in the early stages, is to run your code as often as you can. If you do get an error when you run it, you will have a smaller number of changes since you did the last check, so the debugging process will be much simpler. If you don't, you'll feel encouraged and confident that every-thing is going well.

Great! Now that we are writing good code, let's consider some of the standard questions we have to ask ourselves when we are debugging. These are the most important questions in this whole chapter, and perhaps in the whole of coding itself – if you can answer them, you can fix any problem.

Step 1: The three questions

When a new coder finds that some code they have written doesn't work, they often feel frustrated, not sure where to look to fix the problem, and as a result they often blame themselves ('I'll never be able to do this') or the machine itself ('stupid computer'). This is perfectly natural, and all coders have experienced this emotion many times.

The difference between experienced and novice coders, however, is that the experienced coder knows that this has happened many times before, that it doesn't mean he or she is an idiot, and that it can likely be fixed using the same process they use every time.

So what is this process? The first question to ask is a painfully obvious one: *What makes you say your code isn't working?*

The answer to this question might be frustratingly self-evident: 'My code won't compile!'; 'My website won't display properly'; 'The button doesn't do anything when I press it!'

But forcing yourself to answer this question is harder than you think. If you have an error message, pay careful attention to it – what is it saying? Error messages can often be obscure, but you should be able to extract some meaning from it. It will also often tell you the exact line that the error occurred, which is a great starting point. And 'googling the error message' is a perfectly reasonable (and common) thing to do as a coder!

If you don't have an error message, this can be trickier, but you should at the least clarify exactly what the problem is. Evolving your thinking from 'My website won't display properly' to 'My logo is appearing at the bottom of the screen, but I want it at the top' is a big step forward. With layout issues in particular, dealing with problems one at a time is crucial – it's easy to get overwhelmed, but breaking the issues down into individual errors and getting them clear in your head will make fixing them much easier.

Now that you (hopefully) have a clear understanding of what exactly is not behaving as expected, it's time to move on to question 2: *How is your code supposed to work?*

Again, answering this question might be frustrating – you only wrote the code five minutes ago, you know how it's supposed to work – but all too often running through the part of the code that seems to be causing the problem is all that is needed to fix the issue.

With the logo issue, for example, you would likely go to the CSS that controls the position of the logo. Thinking through the CSS commands you have written, how *should* the logo display? Are there any conflicting lines of CSS that could be changing its position unexpectedly?

If a button is not responding, mentally work through the process that is supposed to happen when the button is clicked. Is the button correctly connected to the function you have written for it? Could there be an error in that function? Does the function actually display a result, or does it just do some calculations without changing the UI at all?

Ninety per cent of code errors should be fixed by now, if you have carefully asked yourself those two questions. If you're not done yet, though, it's time for question 3: *What tweaks can you make to clarify what your code is doing?*

If you have well-written, clearly commented code, it should be fairly obvious what your code is up to at any point. However, even good code can contain mistakes, and our final trick is to play with some variables, or add small lines of code, to see what effect that has on how the app runs or the website displays.

Going back to the logo example, you could try experimenting with some values – does changing the margin-top value move the logo down as you might expect? If not, why not? If you really can't find the error you can always remove all the CSS code except the lines that should be controlling the logo's location. If it then displays correctly, add them back in gradually until the problem recurs. Bingo – you have found the problem.

With our problematic button, try using a 'print' command (more on those shortly) to display the value of a variable to make sure it is what you think it is. You could even just use something like:

```
print("hello");
```

to make sure a certain chunk of code is being executed at all. The code removal process can be useful here as well – try removing all the button execution code apart from a print statement. If the print doesn't happen, then there is a problem in the connection between the button and the code. If it does, add the code in gradually until it stops behaving as you would expect. Then you know where the error is.

Ninety-five per cent of the time your error should now be fixed – the process of defining the problem, explaining to yourself how your code works, and tweaking values/using print statements is the standard process that you should go through each time.

Incidentally, this is exactly the procedure you can often apply to real-life difficulties. Defining the problem is often the hardest part of making a certain process more efficient, or even figuring out why you are unlucky in love. Then, explaining to yourself what you are currently doing and why is probably enough for you to see where you are going wrong. If not, experiment with changing small things and see if that improves the situation.

What if you still have a bug though? Sometimes we simply can't fix a problem ourselves, and need to resort to outside help. Fortunately, because we have clearly defined the problem, and have a strong understanding of what our code is *supposed* to do, we should be able to search for, and ask for, help effectively.

Step 2: Searching for help

If you've got this far in this book, you've almost certainly done some debugging yourself and, in the process of googling for an answer, you've likely come across stackoverflow.com. Stack Overflow is a simple idea – people post questions and other people answer them – but it has proved extremely popular, and combined with a strong search engine, the answer to a huge range of common programming questions is at your fingertips.

But what to search for? As we have mentioned, if you have a particular error message, simply googling that is a good first step. If not, you'll need to think more carefully about what to search for.

As a starting point, always include the name of the programming language and/or platform in your search. A search for 'how do I change the colour of text' could apply to a huge range of different pieces of software, so add 'HTML', 'CSS', 'JavaScript' or 'Swift' at the end to get your answer much more quickly.

With Android development, it is often worth adding both 'Java' and 'Android' to the search term, as Java is used in a range of different devices, and is not just for Android apps.

If you are using a specific development environment, such as Xcode or Android Studio, it can be useful to add this to your search as well. If nothing else, including 'Xcode' in a 'Swift' search makes it less likely that your results will include articles about Taylor Swift!

Beyond that, as with any web search, try to be concise and unambiguous (this should come naturally after asking the three questions).

Here are some bad search queries. Try to think of better alternatives:

• 'How do I make text bigger?'
• 'Swift blank screen on app launch'
• 'No sound in android app'
• 'Image won't display in website'

Some better alternatives might be:

• 'CSS how to change text size'
• 'Xcode Swift [give error message here]'
• 'Java Android how to play sound'
• 'HTML how to display image'

Note that with the last two, instead of searching for the error, we are looking for instructions or code for how to do what we are trying to do. We might then copy and paste the code we find into our app or website to see if that works. If it does, we can compare it to our code to see what is wrong. If it doesn't, we can be fairly sure that the code itself is not the problem, and that the issue lies elsewhere.

A quick caveat on copying and pasting code that you've found on the internet – this is a risky thing to do. At the very least you should make sure that you understand how the code works, but also bear in mind that it could have been written for an older version of your programming environment (Swift in particular is updated regularly), or possibly even for a different setup than the one you are using. In short, only copy and paste short chunks of code that you understand and could debug yourself if necessary.

OK, so we've asked ourselves the questions, we've searched online, and we've come up with nothing. It's time for the programmer's last resort: to ask for help.

Step 3: Asking for help

Programmers are a pretty helpful bunch, and are more willing than most to help out in exchange for some internet points, or just a public thank you. However, they don't like being asked vague questions or questions that have already been answered elsewhere.

If you are on some kind of programming course where you can ask questions, that is obviously a good place to start. When you ask your questions there, make sure you give all the information that someone could need to solve your problem. However, avoid pasting *all your code*, giving the error message and asking what is wrong. This is very time consuming to debug!

Instead, answer the three questions above, telling your potential helpers what you are trying to do, what result you are getting, what debugging you have done, and the *few* lines of code that you have isolated that are causing the problem.

If you don't have access to that sort of forum, stackoverflow.com is probably the best place to ask questions. There is a very helpful guide to asking good questions at http://stackoverflow.com/help/how-to-ask. If you ask your question well, you'll normally have some useful responses within an hour. Not bad!

It goes without saying that when you have an answer to your question, you should always offer a quick 'thank you' (or, on Stack Overflow, 'accept' the correct answer). And when you're further down the line, consider answering some questions yourself to help others get started.

We have now gone through the whole debugging process (the latter stages of which, incidentally, are pretty much identical to the 'How do I...' process, if you're trying to learn how to do something you haven't done before). We'll now look at specific debugging tools for the different languages we have covered. These can save you a lot of time, and make the whole process much smoother.

Debugging HTML and CSS

The most useful tools to most web developers are the Developer Tools, which are included with most browsers. Here we'll look at the Chrome Developer Tools, which we think are the most comprehensive. To access them in Chrome, click View → Developer → Developer Tools.

11.1

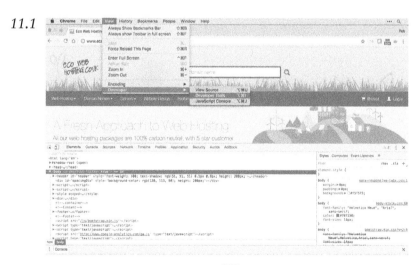

A window will appear at the bottom of the screen – click on the Elements tab and you'll see the HTML of the page you're on and a summary of the CSS styles on the right.

Different sections of the HTML are usually hidden behind '...'s – just click on the... to view them. You can also click the button in the top left of the window to select any element on the page and view the HTML and CSS related to it. Try it out – it's pretty cool.

You can even edit the HTML of the page by double-clicking on it, which can be very useful for debugging individual elements (or changing the headline on cnn.com and impressing your colleagues – of course, this only edits the version stored on your computer, not the live version on CNN's servers!).

A particularly useful CSS trick is to enable and disable individual styles (*11.2*):

11.2

```
@media screen and (min-width: 600px)
.js {                                   main.css:1
  ✅ padding: ▶ 0;
}                                           ⋮
```

Just hover over the style and click the blue tick to disable it. You can also change the values of styles, just as you can with the HTML.

Once you've finished playing with the Elements tab, click on Console. We will be using this more in the JavaScript debugging section, but here it is useful for seeing any errors in the page.

You will also see other major HTML errors here, but if you want to check your HTML in more detail, you can use an HTML Validator, such as https://validator.w3.org/. This will tell you if your page has, for example, unclosed HTML tags, or options for elements that are no longer supported.

This can be very useful, but don't necessarily expect your code to have no errors whatsoever. At the time of writing, www. bbc.co.uk/ had over 100 errors!

When it comes to CSS, http://csslint.net/ is an extremely powerful tool. It will not only show you CSS errors, but also conflicts, where two different styles are conflicting with each other, and also advise you on how your CSS could be better.

Debugging JavaScript

As with HTML and CSS, your main tools for debugging JavaScript are the browser Developer Tools, specifically the Console. Not only will that show you any JavaScript errors, but you can also use it to find out values of variables, or whether certain chunks of code are being run.

Try running this JavaScript on a webpage and looking at the results in the console:

```
for (i = 0; i < 10; i++) {
    console.log(i)
}
```

You should see something like this (11.3):

The console.log command allows us to print something in the console, which is an extremely powerful debugging tool.

Beyond the console, www.jslint.com/ is similar to CSS Lint, and will show you a range of errors and warning messages.

Debugging Swift in Xcode

Xcode, like most integrated development environments (IDEs), has a range of debugging features. The first is inline error messages. It is pretty clear when there is a syntax error, although the error messages themselves can be a challenge to decipher.

If you run some code that causes your app to crash, you'll often see a very unfriendly (and not particularly helpful) 'terminating with uncaught exception of type NSException' message (*11.4*):

11.4

However, scroll up in the console and you'll usually find something useful; in this case we are attempting to print an array value that doesn't exist (*11.5*):

11.5

```
14
15    override func viewDidLoad() {
16        super.viewDidLoad()
17        // Do any additional setup after loading the view, typically from a nib.
18
19        let array = [1, 2, 3]
20
21        print(array[4])
22
23    }
24
25    override func didReceiveMemoryWarning() {
26        super.didReceiveMemoryWarning()
27        // Dispose of any resources that can be recreated.
28    }
```

```
fatal error: Index out of range
(lldb)
```

Xcode's equivalent of console.log in JavaScript is the 'print' function, which works like this:

```
print("Hello World")
```

As with console.log, it allows you to display variable values, or verify that a specific chunk of code is being run. If the console is not visible, you can make it appear by clicking at the top right of the Xcode window.

Debugging Java in Android studio

Android Studio's debugging tools are similar to Xcode's. There is automated error checking, to show you syntax errors and warnings (*11.6*):

11.6
```
int ageInt = Integer.parseInt(age)
```

You do need to look quite carefully as the red wiggly under-score is often not immediately obvious. There is also a red line on the right-hand side of the editing window, and if you hover over either the underscore or the line, you'll be given the error message (*11.7*):

11.7

';' expected —

If you run some code which has errors in it, you'll see errors appear in the logs as with Xcode. There is also the facility to write messages in the logs, similar to console.log and print. To do that, use the Log command, like this:

```
Log.i("Message", "The log command was run");
```

Each log command has a title (in this case 'Message') and content ('The log command was run'). The 'i' in Log.i is short for information, and the command allows you to use different letters for different log types, the most common of which are:

- D – Debug.
- I – Info.
- W – Warning.
- E – Error.

Summary

We have now gone through all the major debugging techniques, and seen a range of tools to debug code on a variety of platforms. We've also seen how to write good code, to minimize the amount of time we spend debugging.

Debugging is a necessary process for any programmer, but done right it can be a learning experience in itself. The most important thing is to approach debugging calmly and methodically, and try to avoid letting the bugs stress you out!

We've also glimpsed how we might apply the debugging methods to life in general, and work tasks in particular. Take a few moments now to approach some of the aspects of your job or life that are currently problematic or inefficient. Ask yourself the three questions and see what difference it makes. You should be pleasantly surprised!

This concludes the 'In Practice' section, in which we have seen how you can apply the coding skills you learned in the previous section to build real websites and apps. We are now going to see how you can further use your coding skills to future-proof your career, starting with using coding to enhance your career prospects.

PART FOUR

Future-proofing your career with coding

CHAPTER TWELVE

Using coding to enhance your career

So far, we have spent most of this book learning to build websites and apps. We hope you have enjoyed learning these skills, but it is likely that you still have your day job, and might be wondering how knowing how to code might benefit you within your current role. This is what we will be considering in this chapter, and by the end of it you should have at least one way in which you can future-proof your career using your newfound talents.

Many employers are desperate for increased digital literacy among their staff. We live in a world dominated by software, but only a minority understand how it works. This has created a skills gap in which companies in all sectors are increasingly desperate to employ highly technical candidates. This means that even if you don't intend to change careers, completing coding-related projects and activities is a great boost for your employability and gives potential employers reasons to hire you. You should always put your coding skills on your CV, stating what languages you have knowledge of, how you are able to put them into practice, what level you are at, and listing any websites, apps or projects you have worked on. Discussing your coding achievements can also be an excellent way to impress at an interview if you're looking for a brand new job. If you want to stand out in your current role, mentioning your abilities to your manager during a catch-up or offering your coding skills to a project will help you succeed at making an impression.

All of the suggestions in this chapter will boost your career prospects by developing and demonstrating your technical abilities. Not all of the suggestions in this chapter will necessarily apply to your role or sector, but you'll be surprised how far a little creative thinking (combined with the coding skills you have learned so far) can take you.

We will start by considering whether you could create an app for the company you work for, and what that app might look like. Next we'll look at the process of starting a blog, and why it is likely you would benefit from having one, regardless of the industry you are working in. Then we'll look at a number of ways you can automate or streamline processes in your daily workflow, using tools such as If This Then That, Text Expansion, AppleScript and PowerShell.

Creating an app for your business

Regardless of the type of company you work for, it is likely that there is a process that could be done better if there was an app created specifically for it. As a teacher, Rob created a simple app to manage house points. Staff could give students a house point instantly, and students could see straight away which house had the most points. What app could you build that would make you or your colleagues' work lives better? (Note – you could probably build a website to do the same job, but we find people get rather more excited about apps than websites!)

Building an app for your company is a great way to learn the complete app development cycle without having to come up with a ground-breaking idea. You can be sure that at least someone will use your app, and with any luck you'll get some kudos for creating it. You might even find yourself becoming the digital guru in your office!

Simple app ideas might include:

- An 'onboarding' app that tells new employees basic information about how things work at your office.
- An 'important information' app containing useful phone numbers, email addresses and other information that all employees would find handy.
- An app that displays information about the business, such as sales figures, circulation or progress towards certain goals.

The most important thing about your first business-focused app (as with any app) is to keep it simple. Make sure it does one thing well rather than trying to solve all the problems your company has in one go.

To give a real-life example, John Williams is a fireman based in the United Kingdom. He realized that in the training of his colleagues there were various tests that needed to be completed, but no centralized system keeping track of who had successfully completed each test. Moreover, fire stations in different districts used different processes. He created a system for his district so that someone could not only take the tests online, but a supervisor could keep track of which tests each of the firemen had passed, and thus knew when to put them forward for the official exam.

Since creating the app, John has been approached by a number of nearby districts to use the app themselves. It's early days yet, but it could become a very useful teaching and learning tool, used by fire stations throughout the United Kingdom.

Creating an app for yourself or your colleagues allows you to 'scratch your own itch', ie solve a problem that you know exists for at least a small number of people because you have that problem yourself. You'll also get quick feedback (good and bad!) from your colleagues, and there is always the possibility your app will grow into something bigger than you could imagine.

Starting a blog

In the world of Facebook and Twitter, writing a blog might feel a little old fashioned. You can certainly develop a following on social media (and we'll look at how to do that more effectively later in this chapter), but running your own blog has a few unique advantages. Firstly, the sheer fact that setting up a blog is more difficult than creating a Facebook or Twitter account shows that you are serious. It is a way of telling the world that you have something to say, and that you are dedicated enough to regularly create content that people enjoy.

Secondly, as it is *your* blog, you have complete control over your content. You are not limited as you are with social networks in how content will be displayed, or who can view it.

Thirdly, and most importantly, there is the *Google effect*. Increasingly, regardless of your industry, potential employers will use search engines to find out about job applicants. If you run and update a blog that will almost certainly become the top search result when people search for you. That's a pretty impressive thing for a potential employer to see.

Fourth, *owning your domain name* is increasingly useful. As we have seen, a domain name is a web address, like google.com. Owning robpercival.co.uk has been very useful for Rob, and we would thoroughly recommend that you stop reading right now and try to purchase your name. If you have a common name, you might need to try alternative domain extensions such as .me, or .blog, or you can get creative like the blogger John Gruber did when he set up his blog at daringfireball.net (which you'll hear more detail about later in this chapter).

Fifth, you can use your blog to build a community and position yourself as an authority figure. If you write useful and challenging content, you will start to build a following of like-minded people who are interested in what you do. By encouraging them to post comments on your articles, you can get to know these people, and form a community with you at the centre. This is a very powerful thing, and a whole range of opportunities might develop from it.

Finally, once you have built up an audience, if you wish you can monetize the blog itself, by offering subscriptions for special content, recommending products, or just using the platform to launch your next big business idea.

There are countless other benefits from writing a blog. You will be forced to write clearly and coherently, expressing your ideas eloquently and in an entertaining way. This is a rare and valuable skill across all industries. It will clarify your thinking and your ideas. It will build your confidence as you write more and your audience grows. It can help bring attention to causes that you care about, and even change public policy. It will bring in new experiences, with new people, and develop your technical and marketing skills. And, of course, you will help people by sharing your knowledge and experiences or simply entertaining them.

Choosing a topic

At this point, you're probably thinking 'I don't have anything to write about.' That's not true. You may not feel particularly unique, but you are the only person in the world with your set of experiences, skills and hobbies. We'd be very surprised if there wasn't something that you care about, know more about than most people, and would like to share with the world.

If you're not sure what you might write about, grab a pen and a blank piece of paper. Write down 20 topics that you are interested in. These might be hobbies, styles of music or art, regions of the world, sport, issues related to your job, charitable or political causes, technology, or anything else. Think about which topics you would be keen to write about, and which you might be in a particularly good position to discuss. The best blog writing is informed and passionate, but those who set up successful blogs are rarely great authorities on their subject. They are just normal people who commit to creating quality content regularly.

If you're still not sure what you might write about, you might just choose to be very honest about your job, sharing what it is like day to day to be an accountant, teacher or airline pilot. Or you could take up a completely new hobby or learn something new and blog about the process. You could even blog about learning to code!

Like starting a business, starting a blog is a little nerve-racking, and requires a leap of confidence to take the first step, but it is incredibly rewarding, and you never know where it might lead.

Blogging success stories

THE CAUSE

There are endless stories of people who have achieved great things through writing blogs. One particularly impressive tale is that of Martha Payne, a nine-year-old from Scotland who created the 'Never Seconds' blog at http://neverseconds.blogspot.co.uk/, writing about the poor quality of her school dinners. Within three months the blog had come to the attention of the national media, and the local authorities quickly started to improve the food at their schools. Martha raised over £100,000 for school children in Malawi, won The Observer Food Blog of the Year award, and went on to publish a book about her experiences. (Book publishing is a common outcome of writing a popular blog, so if that's something that's on your bucket list, there's yet another reason to give it a go.)

THE HOBBY THAT BECAME A FULL-TIME JOB

John Gruber was a software developer from Philadelphia, who launched his Daring Fireball blog in 2002. He writes about whatever interests him, which is primarily Apple-related topics, software development and user interfaces. He is known for writing passionately and clearly, with strong opinions. The popularity of the blog grew gradually until 2010, when one particular post about third-party applications for building iPhone apps was mentioned by Steve Jobs in an email to a user. This controversial topic was covered by the media, and brought Daring Fireball to a massive new level of popularity.

The blog became Gruber's full-time job in 2006, with income coming from sponsorship, advertisements and affiliate links. Affiliate links are links that go to particular products, and when the user buys those or similar products after clicking the link the publisher (in this case Gruber) gets a fixed amount, or a percentage of the purchase. We will talk more about affiliate links later in this section.

Gruber now also runs The Talk Show podcast and has speaking engagements around the world. Like publishing a book, if you have ever wanted to be a professional public speaker, starting a blog is a great first step.

Gruber's story shows that while writing a blog can be slow progress (it took him four years for it to produce a full-time income), you don't need any special authority, experience or insider knowledge to be successful. He was 'just another' software developer that shared his opinions in a way that completely changed his life.

MUDDY STILETTOS

Blogs don't have to offer incisive opinion or shocking truth – they can just be fun. Hero Brown launched http://muddystilettos.co.uk/ in 2011 to help people in Buckinghamshire UK find the best places to dine and shop. By November 2012, the blog had become Brown's full-time job, and has since spread to providing fun first-hand information about restaurants, hotels and country life in nine counties.

These are just three examples of successful blogs, but there are many more. Mrs Cassidy shared what her six-year-old pupils got up to at http://mscassidysclass.edublogs.org/. Mr J. Brown blogs about yoga at www.jbrownyoga.com/, and is building an online workshop on the success of his writing. Mark Lee blogs about accounting at http://marksaccjokes.blogspot.co.uk/, his blog forming the basis of his consultancy and public-speaking business.

Whatever you want to achieve with your career, starting a blog is a great way to begin.

How to start a blog

Creating a blog is much like building any other website, so for buying domain names, getting web hosting and other general topics, refer back to Chapter 7. The main decision you will need to make for your blog is what platform to use. As with web development, there are a selection of blogging platforms that you can use, including wordpress.com, tumblr.com and blogger.com. All of these will allow you to set your blog up quickly, but have the major disadvantage that you do not completely own your content. If you want to move to a different provider, this can be very difficult. You might also be limited to what features you can have, or what styles, layouts and website structures you can use.

Our advice would be to use a self-hosted platform, and by far the most common platform for bloggers is Wordpress. (Note wordpress.com is essentially a hosted version of Wordpress – they offer broadly the same features but with a self-hosted setup you have much greater control over your site.) For advice on setting up a hosting for your Wordpress website, see Chapter 7. Once you have set up the hosting, your hosting provider can guide you how to install Wordpress and the whole process, from buying a domain name to seeing your site live, shouldn't take more than a few hours (and most of that time will be waiting for the website to become live).

While it is possible to create a blog without any coding skills, you will be able to use your HTML and CSS experience to customize the look and feel of your site, rather than relying on the default look of available themes. You can also use JavaScript and other languages to customize the behaviour of your site and add specific functionality, such as a sign-up form or calendar.

We hope by now you are seriously thinking about starting a blog, but if you are not quite ready for that yet there are a number of other ways you can use coding to enhance your career prospects, or just to do your current job more efficiently. We'll start by looking at ways that we can automate or speed up tasks using code.

Finding tasks that can be automated

In almost every job there is a part of the workflow that can be done more efficiently. If your job is marketing, you may well end up posting the same thing to Twitter, Facebook, and perhaps other social networks. If you write lots of emails, you might find that you type the same phrases, sentences or paragraphs over and over. In researching a book, you might want to collect email addresses from a number of websites. You may need to rename a large number of files. Or you may have a list of files, and need to search through them for specific words. We'll see how to automate each of these tasks, and look at more general use-cases for the tools that we create.

If This Then That

If This Then That (https://ifttt.com/) is a web service that allows you to connect a huge range of other apps and automate various processes. Each process is known as an 'applet', and range from 'save all photos I am tagged in on Facebook to Dropbox' to 'send me an email when it's going to rain'. But there are a range of more useful applets, in particular 'Post your tweets to Facebook when you use a specific hashtag' (https://ifttt.com/applets/112202p-post-your-tweets-to-facebook-when-you-use-a-specific-hashtag). This solves our first problem, and if managing social media accounts is part of your job, this can save a huge amount of time.

You might even find tasks that you don't currently do, but could be done automatically and benefit your business. If you use Mailchimp to send newsletters for example, you can automatically share the latest newsletters' performance with your colleagues via email, Slack and a Google Spreadsheet (https://ifttt.com/applets/DHFQvPEj-share-newsletter-performance-with-the-team).

While not coding as such, using IFTTT forces you to think through the conditions that you want to cause your applet to run, and exactly what output you want, and so it involves many of the same challenges. More importantly, it can make your life a lot easier, and dramatically increase your productivity, so take a little time to look at the applets available, and think about how you could apply them in your current role.

Text expansion

A lot of jobs require you to write similar phrases and sentences frequently, often many times a day. At the very least you might need to type your email address, phone number or home address pretty regularly. Text expansion allows you to assign shortcodes to any text, so you might assign 'wyt' to 'What do you think?'

In some text expansion apps, you can even use shortcodes to insert images, or press buttons like Tab or Enter. You can use this to log into a site with just a shortcode, by instructing the short-code to insert your email address, then 'press' the Tab key to move you to your password field, insert your password, and then press Tab to move to the Login button and then press Enter to log in.

How much time this will save depends on your role, but there are few people that wouldn't benefit from setting up a few basic phrases.

TEXT EXPANSION ON MACOS

Text expansion is actually built into MacOS, so you don't need to download any extra software, unless you want advanced features. To access it, click the Apple icon in the top left of the screen and then select System Preferences and Keyboard. Select the 'Text' tab and you'll see the Keyboard Shortcuts window.

Just use the + button to add new shortcodes and you're done!

TEXT EXPANSION ON WINDOWS

There is no built-in text expansion utility for Windows, but Phrase Express (www.phraseexpress.com) has a free edition for personal use and Word Expander (www.wordexpander.net/) is completely free.

If you want to investigate more advanced features, the full versions of Phrase Express, as well as the cross-platform Text Expander (https://textexpander.com/) are both excellent places to start. Like with IFTTT, while text expansion is not coding as such it still requires you to think carefully about how you want the app to behave, and if you use some of the advanced features it can get pretty complex. Give it a try now, and see how much time you can save.

Using Python to extract email addresses from a website

The process of extracting information from websites automatically is known as 'scraping', and is widely used in Python. It can save a lot of time when researching the web if you want to, for example, gather a collection of email addresses or the titles of a range of books or blog posts. Python is great for this sort of thing, and we have included below a simple web scraper, which 'crawls' the web, starting from a certain page. Crawling is the process of downloading a number of different webpages, by looking for links on the original page. In this case, we start with www.ecowebhosting.co.uk; look for all the links on that page, download the content from each of those pages, and then search for email addresses on that page. It uses Beautiful Soup (www.crummy.com/software/BeautifulSoup/), a Python library designed to make website scraping easier.

The code is a slightly edited version of http://scraping.pro/simple-email-crawler-python/. It is well commented, and uses rather more advanced Python than we have seen so far, so we won't go through it line by line, but if you have some ideas of how you could use web scraping in your job, you should be able to figure out how it works using the comments. You can then customize it to your precise needs.

```python
from bs4 import BeautifulSoup
import requests
import requests.exceptions
from urllib.parse import urlsplit
from collections import deque
import re

# a queue of urls to be crawled
new_urls = deque(['http://www.ecowebhosting.co.uk'])

# a set of urls that we have already crawled
processed_urls = set()

# a set of crawled emails
emails = set()

# process urls one by one until we exhaust the queue
```

```
while len(new_urls):
        # move next url from the queue to the set of
          processed urls
        url = new_urls.popleft()
        processed_urls.add(url)

        # extract base url to resolve relative links
        parts = urlsplit(url)
        base_url = "{0.scheme}://{0.netloc}".
        format(parts)
        path = url[:url.rfind('/')+1] if '/' in parts.
          path else url

        # get url's content
        print("Processing %s" % url)
        try:
        response = requests.get(url)
        except (requests.exceptions.MissingSchema,
          requests.exceptions.ConnectionError):
        # ignore pages with errors
        continue

        # extract all email addresses and add them into
          the resulting set
        new_emails = set(re.findall(r"[a-z0-9\.\-+_]+@
          [a-z0- 9\.\-+_]+\.[a-z]+", response.text, re.I))
        emails.update(new_emails)
# create a beautiful soup for the html document
soup = BeautifulSoup(response.text)

# find and process all the anchors in the document
for anchor in soup.find_all("a"):
        # extract link url from the anchor
```

```
link = anchor.attrs["href"] if "href" in anchor.
  attrs else "
# resolve relative links
if link.startswith('/'):
link = base_url + link
elif not link.startswith('http'):
link = path + link
# add the new url to the queue if it was not
  enqueued nor processed yet
if not link in new_urls and not link in processed_
urls:

new_urls.append(link)
```

Automation on MacOS

If there is a task on your computer that you do regularly, such as exporting video files, or saving Photoshop files in specific resolutions, it's likely that you can automate it. Here we will see how to do that on both MacOS and Windows.

All Mac computers come with AppleScript built in. This is a special programming language that you can use to open apps, click menu items, type text and a lot more. To begin with AppleScript, use cmd-space to open Spotlight and type in 'Script Editor'. This will open the MacOS AppleScript Editor.

This is a simple program that allows you to create and edit AppleScripts. To give an example of how AppleScript works, here is a script that bulk-renames a set of files.

The code comes from https://gist.github.com/oliveratgithub/b9030365c9ae483984ea, and as before is well commented (comments in AppleScript being with '--') so just read through to see how it works:

```
set text item delimiters to "."

tell application "Finder"

set all_files to every item of (choose file with prompt
"Choose the Files you'd like to rename:" with multiple
selections allowed) as list

display dialog "New file name:" default answer ""

set new_name to text returned of result

--now we start looping through all selected files.
'index' is our counter that we initially set to 1 and
then count up with every file.

--the 'index' number is of course required for the
sequential renaming of our files!

repeat with index from 1 to the count of all_files

--using our index, we select the appropriate file from
our list

set this_file to item index of all_files

set file_name_count to text items of (get name of this_
file)

--if the index number is lower than 10, we will add a
preceding "0" for a proper filename sorting later

if index is less than 10 then

set index_prefix to "0"

else

set index_prefix to ""
```

```
end if

--

--let's check if the current file from our list (based
on index-number) has even any file-extension

if number of file_name_count is 1 then

--file_name-count = 1 means, we extracted only 1 text-
string from the full file name. So there is no file-
extension present.

set file_extension to ""

else

--yup, we are currently processing a file that has a
file-extension

--we have to re-add the original file-extension after
changing the name of the file!

set file_extension to "." & item -1 of file_name_count

end if

--let's rename our file, add the sequential number from
'index' and add the file-extension to it

set the name of this_file to new_name & index_prefix &
index & file_extension as string

end repeat

--congratulations for successfully accomplishing the
batch renaming task:)

display alert "All done! Renamed " & index & " files
with '" & new_name & "' for you. Have a great day!:)"

end tell
```

To try the script out, copy and paste it into the Script Editor, and click File → Export. Change the File Format to Application and call the app 'Bulk Renamer'.

You can then run the app and the renaming will take place. If there are any repetitive tasks that are part of your regular workflow, see if you could write an AppleScript app to automate the process.

Automation on Windows

The equivalent to AppleScript on Windows is PowerShell. PowerShell 5.0 is included with Windows 10, so let's use it to see how we could search through a collection of files looking for a particular snippet of text.

To open PowerShell, just type 'PowerShell' into the search bar at the bottom left of the screen.

The code below comes from http://www.adminarsenal.com/admin-arsenal-blog/powershell-searching-through-files-for-matching-strings/, and again should be fairly self-explanatory (comments in PowerShell start with '#').

```
##############################################################
$Path = "C:\temp"
$Text = "This is the data that I am looking for"
$PathArray = @()
$Results = "C:\temp\test txt"

# This code snippet gets all the files in $Path that
end in ".txt".
Get-ChildItem $Path -Filter "*.txt" |
Where-Object { $_.Attributes -ne "Directory"} |
ForEach-Object {
```

```
If (Get-Content $_.FullName | Select-String -Pattern
$Text) {
$PathArray += $_.FullName
$PathArray += $_.FullName
}
}
Write-Host "Contents of ArrayPath:"
$PathArray | ForEach-Object {$_}
####################################################
```

As with MacOS, if you regularly complete repetitive tasks on a Windows machine, take some time to consider if writing a PowerShell script would make you more efficient.

Summary

In this chapter you have a seen a range of ways that you can use coding to enhance your career prospects. You've considered building an app for your company, starting a blog, and using a variety of tools to make your workflow more automated and efficient. We hope you've taken away at least one of these ideas and used it to improve your work life.

We're now going to take the next step – to consider how you might use your coding skills to launch a product or a business. This could be as simple as creating and selling a digital product such as an ebook or video course, or building the next big social network. We will lead you through the process from idea-creation to marketing and growing the business.

## CHAPTER THIRTEEN

Coding and entrepreneurship

One of the most exciting things about learning to code is that it enables you to create your own business, product or service, and allows people around the world to access it immediately. This is something that has only been possible in the last 20 years or so, and has brought the cost of starting a business down to close to zero.

We've already seen how to create and host a website, and how to build apps for Android and iOS. In this chapter we will walk you through the process of starting an online business using your newfound skills. As always, this chapter is practical, so keep a pen and paper handy to jot down ideas and business plans as you read through the chapter.

Aim to come up with and test at least one business idea by the end of the chapter. You might not become the next Mark Zuckerberg or Bill Gates, but at the least you should be able to build a second income stream, and you'll certainly have a lot of fun, and learn a great deal, along the way.

We will begin by seeing how you can generate business ideas, and where the best ideas come from. We'll then go on to see how you can validate and hone your ideas, making sure that the one you choose is most likely to succeed. Finally we'll look at creating your initial product, getting it to customers, and pricing.

What's coding got to do with entrepreneurship?

Many of the examples and suggestions below have little to do with coding, so you might be wondering why you would need to code at all to start a business. The answer is of course that you can start a business without learning to code, but being able to code makes the whole process *so much easier*.

Not only do you have a better understanding of how the websites and services you are using function, enabling you to use them more effectively, but if you cannot code you will constantly come up against frustrating challenges. If your business needs a website, you can just create it rather than paying someone else, or paying for a hosted service. If your business needs an app, or a mailing list, or an automated process, you can just build it, which is extremely liberating.

Even if you decide not to build your own website or app, knowing the basics of coding means you'll be able to communicate effectively with whomever is doing so, resulting in a much better, and likely cheaper, outcome.

Getting ideas

Every great business starts with an idea. Ideas can come from anywhere, but in our experience the most reliably successful way to choose an idea is to choose a niche that you are already familiar with. *Scratch your own itch* is a phrase we have seen before, and if something is a pain-point for you, it likely is for a number of other people as well.

For example, if you are a yoga instructor and find it difficult to get clients because there is no central portal where people can search for and rate different yoga instructors, perhaps creating that portal would be a good idea.

Or perhaps you are a plumber who finds the process of invoicing and arranging payments from your clients a hassle. Would an automated service, specifically designed for plumbers, be useful to you? If so, it would likely be useful to many others as well.

Don't worry about a niche appearing too small – once you have developed 'traction' (ie a number of people are actively using your service), there are almost always possibilities for expanding into related fields. The yoga portal could grow to support any sporting activity, and the plumbing invoicing service could be applied to a range of domains.

Hopefully a few ideas are already popping into your head, so let's take a moment to choose ideas even more effectively. While it is important (although not crucial) that you have some special knowledge or experience in the business niche, there are two other factors that will substantially affect your chances of success.

The first is whether you have particular skills that will help you be able to succeed with a particular idea where others would not. You should ask yourself *what special skills do I have that mean that I can build this business better than anyone else?* By this we don't mean that you must have finely honed business instincts, but that your capabilities match those required for that particular business. If your idea is going to require a lot of public speaking, and the thought of doing that terrifies you, you might not be best placed to run that business. If you are particularly creative, look for business ideas that will allow you to use your creativity. If you enjoy working with numbers, look for ideas where numbers are critical to its success.

The second factor is what you enjoy doing. Usually people enjoy what they are good at, so often the two overlap, but not always. Rob loves singing and playing the guitar, but he's yet to make a career out of it. But you are much more likely to succeed if you actually enjoy the tasks that will be required of you to create and grow that particular idea. So for each idea, imagine yourself going ahead with it and actually doing the day-to-day activities. Do they seem fun to you? If so, you'll be much more likely to make a success of the business.

You can think of these three factors as a Venn diagram, in which the perfect business idea for you lies in the centre, at the overlap of your skills, experiences and what you enjoy doing (*13.1*).

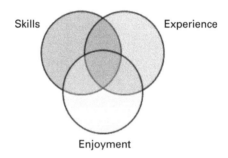

Take a few minutes now to think about business ideas based on your own personal experience – they could relate to your job, hobbies or any aspect of your life. Brainstorm as many ideas as possible – aim for at least 20. Most ideas will appear crazy, ridiculous or impossible at first, but get them down anyway as crazy ideas can often be the seed of a very sensible business.

START-UP STORY

Alice Hall was 27 in 2012, and was struggling to pay her bills. On a whim, she bought £90 of dresses and resold them online. They sold quickly, and she used the profits to buy £180 of dresses. Again, they sold well, and she carried on buying and selling dresses until she was ready to create her own website,

---

pinkboutique.co.uk. As of June 2016, the business had a turnover of £7 million, selling 2,000 dresses a day all round the world. You don't need extensive business experience or a big upfront investment to build a successful business, you just need to start.

Products vs services

It is important to draw a distinction between product- and service-based businesses, as both have quite specific advantages and disadvantages.

A service-based business might be a web hosting company, or a platform for finding good cleaners. Google, Facebook and Vodafone are service-based businesses. Services have the huge advantage of the potential for *recurring revenue*. This is when a customer pays a regular fee for an ongoing service. Having recurring revenue is extremely powerful because you can rely on a certain amount coming in each month. And as your user base grows, it naturally adds to your income for the long term. Of course, you need to provide value for your users for as long as they are paying you, but if you can do that a recurring revenue stream is a boon for any business.

A product-based business might be an ebook, a video course, or reselling dresses. Apple, John Lewis and L'Oréal are primarily product-based businesses. They can be easier to set up, because you don't need to create a complex service for your users. It is also potentially easier to differentiate yourself from competitors, especially if you are the only business that sells your particular product. However, recurring revenue is less likely with a product-based business, and you will need to continually create new products to bring in new income.

Both types of business can be successful, but it is worth being clear what type your idea is. Take a few minutes to divide the ideas you wrote down into product and service businesses, and think about the potential for recurring revenue, or how you will grow the business by creating new products.

Some example ideas

If you're still short of ideas, remember that your first business is unlikely to be your most successful. In the early stages, the important thing is to try *something*. You *will* make mistakes, and there is only so much you can learn from books, so it's best to get out there and start making those mistakes now. Even if your business is not successful, you will have learned a huge amount, about coding, marketing and how to make something people love.

So here are a few simple ideas for your very first business that almost anyone can try. Each of them will require you to test the market, create a product or service, and then actively promote it – the three core skills of starting any business.

AN EBOOK

We're not suggesting you should write a great novel, but creating an ebook is much the same process as starting a business. Choosing a subject, you should look at something that you could write confidently and competently about, and ideally take a unique angle on. It doesn't have to be a masterpiece, but should provide useful information that people are actively looking for. You can publish an ebook for free on Amazon.

A VIDEO COURSE

Various websites now allow you to upload and sell video courses, including udemy.com, stackskills.com and videodirect.amazon. com. As with ebooks, choose a topic that there is a market for, and that you could teach well.

A WORDPRESS PLUGIN OR THEME

We have already seen that Wordpress powers 25 per cent of the web. Therefore there is a huge potential market for add-ons and extras. There are also well-established platforms for providing your products directly to Wordpress users. Themes are available at wordpress.org/themes/, and if you have a good eye you could easily create a popular theme. While all the themes on that page are free, you could charge for extra features, or sell your themes directly on sites like themeforest.net.

Wordpress plugins (wordpress.org/plugins/) add extra functionality to Wordpress, and you can find plugins that do almost anything, from speeding up your website to creating a new social network. As with themes, create a plugin that offers a new feature, or has better integration or a smoother user interface than the existing options.

Your unique selling point

It is important to establish your *unique selling point*, or USP, for your business idea. This is the one reason that people should choose your product or service rather than anyone else's. It might be because the product itself is higher quality, or faster, or better looking. Or your service might have some unique features that aren't available anywhere else. Or it might be something tangential to the main business, such as customer service.

For each of the business ideas you've written down so far, write down what the USP would be. If you can't think of one, it's likely that that idea will not go far.

When should you start your business?

At the beginning of Rob's business career he used what he calls the scatter-gun approach. He would have what he thought was a fantastic idea (or at least better than an existing company). He would say 'If only my business could be 1% the size of [insert big company here], I'd be sorted.' He would then run off and build the website, only to find out that getting customers was harder than he thought, or the service wasn't as popular as he'd hoped. He would then get another fantastic idea and move on to that one.

The downside of this approach is that you will inevitably spend a lot of time on businesses that end up unsuccessful. Having said that, Rob learned a lot (and made a lot of mistakes) with those businesses, and when eventually he hit upon an idea that was successful, he was able to apply the lessons he'd learned and not make those mistakes again.

In short, there is nothing wrong with just going on there and creating the website or product that you are thinking about, and seeing what happens. However, there is a smarter way that will help you establish whether your idea is a good one before going to the trouble of actually building it.

Validating your idea

How do you know if your idea is a good one? This is often a very difficult question to answer but there are a few general techniques you can use.

Firstly, don't listen to your friends and family, unless they have particular skills or experience in your niche. Friends and family generally want you to be happy, and will be keen to encourage you on your new mission, and as a result are not a reliable guide as to whether the idea is a good one or not. Discuss it with them by all means, but 'all my friends said it is a great idea' is not a good enough reason to start.

A good place to begin is to look for potential competitors. Go to Google and enter the keywords that you would expect your future customers to enter if they were looking for your product or service. In our examples above, 'find a yoga instructor' or 'invoicing for plumbers' would be a good start. See what is available already, and take some time to analyse how good these products or services are.

Don't be disheartened if the brilliant idea you had already exists. That just means there is a market for it. It's very unlikely that you'll come up with a completely new idea – the real challenge is to execute your idea better than anyone else. When you analyse the existing businesses, try and get clear in your mind what you could do better. What is the crux of your idea that makes it better than the competition? Perhaps they have poor websites, or bad customer service, or odd pricing.

At the same time, what can you learn from your competitors? What are they doing well that you could incorporate into your business? Don't be afraid to steal great ideas!

What if you don't find any competitors? It could of course mean that you have come up with a genuinely new idea, but not necessarily. It may well mean that there simply isn't a market for your idea, or that people have tried and failed (or that you are searching with the wrong keywords).

Once you have done your competitor research, you should have a fairly clear idea of what makes your business unique, and better than the competition. So now it's time to build it, right? Not yet. First you need to reach some potential customers and talk to them about whether they would want your product or service.

At this point, you can hopefully see another benefit of having a blog, or some sort of online following. If these people were your target market, you could contact them individually or collectively to get their feedback.

If you don't have easy access to potential customers or users, the process will be a little harder, but not impossible. If you are targeting a specific niche, find out where these people are (both in real life and virtually). Find a few in your local area and offer to buy them a coffee or lunch in exchange for feedback on your idea. If there are forums or Facebook groups dedicated to people in your niche, post there.

Face-to-face feedback is particularly valuable, as internet comments can tend towards the flippant and critical. When you are speaking to clients, if at all possible try to get a firm commitment. If you ask 'Would you use this?', they will almost certainly say yes, for the same reason friends and family want to support you. Asking 'How much would you pay for this?' is often more revealing. You could even ask them for a payment then and there (refundable if they are not happy with the product), to establish just how keen they are.

What if you don't have a specific niche, or you have no way of getting in touch with potential customers? One great solution is to create a simple 'Coming Soon' website, and ask people to sign up to your newsletter if they are interested. Include the key features of the product and a rough date when you plan to launch, and perhaps some screenshots if you have any. You could do this with a Wordpress theme, using a service such as mailchimp.com to manage the email sign-ups.

Once you have built your site, tell your friends and family about it and ask them to share it. You could even run a small ad campaign to drive traffic to the site – spending £100 on Google or Facebook ads could be money well spent if it saves you hours building a website no-one wants.

The crucial thing at each stage is to evaluate your idea objectively. Don't be put off if one person tells you it will never work, but at the same time it's likely not wise to 'keep the faith' in the face of overwhelming evidence that there is not a market for your product, or that market is currently served very well by existing businesses.

Creating a minimum viable product

All right, so you are convinced that there is a target market for your product or service, and that you are able to create something better than anything that currently exists? Great. It's time to get to work!

The phrase 'minimum viable product' (MVP) neatly expresses the idea that you should build the smallest thing that you can that will satisfy your customers. It is tempting for budding entrepreneurs to feel that their website or app has to do *everything* – it has to have more features, be better looking, and be easier to use than anything else available. Sometimes this is true, but in most cases it's more important to do one thing extremely well, than it is to do everything your customers need.

Google is a classic example. Their homepage had (and, largely, still has) a simple search box and two buttons. The one thing they did really well was help people find the information they were looking for. Not all businesses can be quite that minimal, but when designing your product you should try to establish what the one thing is that your business does better than anyone else, and focus on that.

The big advantage of the MVP approach is that you can get something in the hands of your users as early as possible. As they say in Silicon Valley, if you are not embarrassed about your product at launch, you launched too late. This is not to say that you should release a half-baked product, but you should focus on releasing as early as possible, rather than adding extra features. That way, you can get feedback from real users from the beginning, meaning that you'll be adding features that they actually want, rather than ones you think they want.

How much to charge?

Pricing is often a very difficult subject for entrepreneurs, and of course the best thing to do varies dramatically depending on what you are providing, and to whom.

The best piece of advice we've ever heard on how much to charge is *don't compete on price*. This doesn't mean that you shouldn't make your pricing competitive, but if your USP is 'we are cheaper', that will likely not be enough in itself to make your business take off.

The simplest way to choose your pricing is to charge a similar amount to your competitors. Charging less will not necessarily help you grow as much as you might think. Firstly, if people think of your business as the cheaper option, it might be difficult to convince them that you are also better. Secondly, if you charge less you will inevitably attract the sort of customer that is relatively price-sensitive. They will then be more likely to leave if a cheaper (or even free) service becomes available. Ideally, you want people to use your business because you offer something better than they can get elsewhere – that way you will build a loyal base of users who love your product.

Do things that don't scale

In today's relatively mature business environment, it can be difficult to see how you can compete with big businesses, who can devote much more time and money to creating a great product. The first answer to this is to focus on a niche that is too small for big businesses to be interested in. The second is to 'do things that don't scale'; that is, spend time making your customers happy in a way that would be impossible in a large business.

In Rob's company Eco Web Hosting, the apparent USP was that the hosting was environmentally friendly. But when he asked people what they liked most about the company, what they usually said was the service. Because he ran the company himself and provided all the support, they were always dealing with the person who knew exactly how the website worked, who was the one who would fix all the problems, and who could make decisions about special discounts or extra services. This is something that big hosting companies with their first-line, second-line and third-line support departments, couldn't match.

START-UP STORY

In the summer of 2008, Joe Gebbia and Brian Chesky couldn't pay their high San Francisco rent. They decided to rent out three air mattresses on their floor and serve breakfast. Three people showed up, paying $80 each. They thought this might be a big idea, so they built a website allowing people to share their spare rooms. The company got two bookings after their initial 'big launch', and made around $800 per month for several months.

The founders realized that most people judged the properties on the photos, and most of the photos on the website were not great. So they bought a fancy camera, and visited individual houses that were listed on the site, offering to take photos for them for free. This took a lot of time and effort, but slowly they started to grow, eventually becoming the multibillion dollar company that Airbnb is today.

Taking photos of their users' rooms is obviously something that they wouldn't be able to do at scale, but in the short term it made all the difference. Is there something you could do to make your business or service stand out, even if it wouldn't scale?

Summary

We hope by now that you've identified the best idea from the list that you wrote at the beginning of this chapter, and that you are looking forward to testing it out and creating your MVP. Starting a business is one of the most exciting things you can do, and will teach you a huge amount about the world, and yourself.

We are now going to move on to see how you might proceed if you wanted to pursue coding further and actually become a web or app developer. Even if you're not planning on a career change, we would recommend reading this final chapter, as we will also cover how to earn a side income from coding by freelancing. This is something anyone can do, regardless of your current role and, like starting a company, is a great way to improve both your coding and business skills.

## CHAPTER FOURTEEN

Pursuing coding further to become a developer

Having considered how you can use your newfound coding skills to advance your career, and start your own business, we will now look at becoming a professional developer. Full-time coders are highly sought-after, well remunerated and have the flexibility of working in a range of industries solving a variety of problems. It is also a career that you can dip your toe into by freelancing or completing small projects at the same time as your main career.

We'll start by establishing whether a career in coding is right for you, and then go on to see how you can get into the sector. We'll look at what languages and platforms to learn, how to build a portfolio and what you should have on your CV. Finally we'll look at applying for both freelance and full-time jobs.

A summary of this chapter would simply be to get experience of as much as you can. Apply for some freelance jobs, learn a range of languages, and practise by building real apps and websites. Not only will you learn fastest this way, but you'll build a portfolio quickly, and find out which aspects of the work you enjoy, and which you don't.

Should you become a full-time coder?

As we've mentioned, becoming a developer is for many a great career choice. Coders are well paid, often have a fair amount of freedom within their role, and spend their days solving problems. If that sounds like something you would enjoy, read on!

Of course, as with any career, coding has its downsides. You'll start at the bottom, and while your income will by no means be meagre, it will take a few years before you can command the top salaries. The work can also be stressful, as managers might not have a strong grasp of the difficulties of the problems they are asking you to solve. Deadlines can be tight, and hours long, depending on the company you work for.

Broadly speaking, there are two main career paths for a coder. You could simply get better and better at your craft, working at a higher level solving more difficult problems. If, while reading this book, you have found yourself researching some of the finer points of the languages we have covered, and trying to establish how they work, this will likely be a great route for you. The best coders can earn great salaries, and will often be headhunted to join new start-ups, with potentially lucrative stock options.

The other option is to take the more management-focused route. After several years coding, you might find that your time is better spent training or managing others, and gradually you will do less programming and more working with people. This path is perhaps better suited to those who enjoy coding, but also appreciate working with people and having more control over the direction of a project.

Of course, only you can decide if a career as a developer is for you, but fortunately it is very easy to try out coding as a career by doing small projects and freelance work. Before we see how to get freelance gigs, let's take a moment to think about what languages and platforms you should focus on.

What languages should you learn?

If you have gone through all the exercises in this book, you will already be familiar with a range of languages. For front-end web development (that is, code to create and manipulate webpages), we have learned HTML, CSS and JavaScript. We learned Python for back-end, or server-side, development. For apps, we covered Swift for iOS apps, and Java for Android. We even looked briefly at AppleScript and PowerShell for automation. That's not a bad selection!

Our hope from having covered all of these is that you should have some idea of which type of development you prefer. You might want to be a jack-of-all-trades, and build both apps and websites, in which case you should simply learn what you need to build your next project.

Web development

If you want to focus on web development, which is probably the most broad area in terms of sheer numbers of jobs and projects available, there are a couple more languages we would recommend investigating. The first is PHP, which is the most widely used server-side language. It is what Wordpress is written in, and is an extremely quick way to build a simple site.

The second is MySQL, which is a database language. We haven't discussed databases yet in this book, but they are a critical component of most websites and apps, and they are used to store data, such as usernames, passwords and user content. The most typical simple website would use HTML, CSS and

JavaScript on the front-end, and PHP and MySQL on the back-end. As a result, a rudimentary knowledge of PHP and MySQL is a necessity for any web developer.

There are of course a whole range of further languages and frameworks you can learn for web development. jQuery is a commonly used JavaScript library that makes working with JavaScript a lot easier. If you enjoyed the Python section, you should look at Django, a popular framework for building websites with Python. Ruby is another server-side language that is increasing in popularity. C# and MS SQL Server are also very prevalent especially in business applications and development.

Beyond these basics, our advice would very much be to learn languages and platforms as needed – build websites for yourself and others, and as you develop the need for a new feature or structure, search the web and see what you find. Let the tools fit the project, not the other way around.

App development

If you want to build apps, your choices are a little more restricted, and although there are other options available, unless you have strong reason to do so we would advise sticking with the languages and IDEs (integrated development environments) covered in this book. That is Swift and Xcode for iOS development, and Java and Android Studio for Android.

These are the most straightforward, and most documented, ways to build apps for iOS and Android, so becoming an expert in those languages and IDEs would be strongly advised if you want to build apps.

If you're not sure which direction you would like to go in, just keep an open mind and keep building things. It is likely that you will develop a preference for, or get offered a job in, one particular platform and set of languages, but if that hasn't happened yet don't worry about it – just keep on learning.

Getting freelance jobs

One of the great advantages of coding as a career choice is that you can start to earn money from it straight away as a freelancer. Even if you have relatively little coding experience, you should be able to find jobs that suit your level. Of course, never claim to be able to complete a job that you won't be able to, but at the same time don't underestimate yourself. Be confident when looking for freelance work, and commit to doing a great job for your client.

When you are just setting out on a freelance career, there is one important thing to remember: in the early days, you are not primarily there to earn money. This may sound strange, but it's true: your primary goals should be to learn your craft and build a portfolio. Those two things are far more valuable than whatever you might earn from a freelance gig, so think of any money you earn as a bonus.

Think of getting freelance work as a free Coding MBA. Instead of paying tens of thousands of pounds for lectures on business techniques and writing essays, you are learning a craft and getting practical business experience for free. Any money you receive in the early months is icing on the cake.

This is important to remember because without a substantial portfolio and significant experience you will likely not be able to charge a great deal for your work. So be prepared to put the hours in now, knowing that the big rewards will come later.

With any work you do, make sure to get a review from the client, ideally on a central platform such as linkedin.com, as references are extremely useful for getting both freelance and full-time work later on. A lesser-known but very powerful place to put reviews is Google Maps – if you set up your business as a local one (using your home address is fine, but you could also use the address of a local shared working space if you ask their permission), you can ask your clients to post reviews there.

Not many developers do this, so when people do local searches for web and app developers, it is likely with just a small number of five-star reviews you could be the top result.

There are two primary ways to get freelance work – locally, or in-person, and using freelance websites.

Getting local freelance jobs

The obvious place to begin looking for local work is with your current social circle. Think about colleagues, friends and family – do any of them have a website that needs updating, or an app idea they would like to build? At this point you may offer to work for free, or in exchange for co-ownership of the website or app, but don't be afraid of charging a fair price if you do a job for a profit-making business.

Another good place to find work is in local meet-ups – go to meetup.com and see what is available in your local area. Most towns and cities have a number of weekly networking events – if yours doesn't perhaps you could set one up. When you go along, be friendly and helpful (and don't be afraid to introduce yourself as a developer!). It is likely some work will come your way, for which you should certainly charge. Do a great job for a good price and don't be surprised when others start seeking you out.

Getting freelance work online

Local freelance jobs are a great place to start, but the market can be limited and highly competitive. Fortunately, there are a number of websites such as upwork.com or freelancer.com where you can bid for freelance jobs all round the world.

The competition is strong, and it may take a few attempts before you get your first paid gig, but remember that you have a few crucial advantages over the more experienced developers on those sites:

- You're primarily there to learn. Your first job may take you three hours and earn you $10, but that's fine because you will have learned a great deal about communicating with clients, fixing website code and bidding for a project. Not only that, but you will have earned your first five-star review (a proud moment)!

- You can take your time. Most developers on those sites post generic bids on a large number of projects. You're still learning, so you can take your time and post a thoughtful, relevant bid that shows that you've actually read the details of the post. Believe me, bids like that are few and far between.

- You can use geography to your advantage. If you live in the United States or Europe, make the most of this by offering to speak to the client on the phone, and using polished English when bidding and replying to messages. By doing this, you'll stand out from the competition.

- You can go the extra mile. As you're there to learn, you can do more than what the client asked for without worrying about the extra time spent. If you're setting up Wordpress, install a caching plugin for them to speed up their site. If you're making a webform, use some custom CSS to make it beautiful. Reply quickly and thoroughly to all their questions, and earn their gratitude.

We will say it again – you will earn money here, but that is your secondary goal. Primarily, you're here to learn how to do freelance web development, and build up your online portfolio and positive reviews.

Pick a freelance site, and stick with it

The hardest part of getting your first gig will be overcoming your lack of positive reviews. For that reason, we would advise picking one freelance site and sticking with it, at least for now. You can join another later, but once you've got three five-star reviews on freelancer.com, you'll find it much easier to find work there than you will with an empty profile on elance.com.

We won't go into the strengths and weaknesses of each freelance site, as these can change dramatically over time. We'd simply advise that you check out a few of them and pick whichever site you like the look of. Check that you can receive funds in your country and that you are happy with their payment terms, and sign up – don't waste a lot of time going through all the sites. We've had the most experience with freelancer.com, so we're going to focus on that site, but the others all work in a similar way.

Here's our list of sites you should check out:

- upwork.com
- freelancer.com
- peopleperhour.com
- guru.com
- craigslist.com

A really useful comparison of these and other sites is available online at www.freshbooks.com/blog/2013/01/16/freelance-jobs. It's focused on writing rather than web development but the same principles apply.

Creating your profile

Once you've picked which site you want to work with, you need to sign up and create your profile. When you create your profile, use the following tips:

- *Use your real identity.* You'll want all the parts of your online presence to tie together, so use your real name, upload a photo and talk about yourself.
- *Be honest.* Don't claim to have skills you don't have. At this stage 'Proficient in HTML, CSS and JavaScript' would suffice, and you can then add further skills as needed.
- *Link to your Twitter feed.* If the freelance site allows, put in a link to your Twitter feed – this will add authority to your profile and reassure prospective clients that you are a genuine

developer. If you don't have a Twitter account, set one up – in the early days it will increase clients' confidence in you, and as your community and following grow it can be a source of work in itself.

- *Complete the exams.* Most freelance sites have 'exams' that you can take both in language (English being the most useful) and various coding languages. They usually cost around $50, but are worth it to get you off the ground when you don't have any reviews.

Bidding for gigs

Initially, look for small, relatively straightforward gigs, with a maximum of $50. Updating websites, fixing broken layouts and adding small features are all common requests. Bid on as many projects as you can, bearing the following in mind:

- *Keep your bid low.* Remember you're here to learn and build your reputation. Keep your bid low, especially when you have zero reviews. This will get you gigs more quickly and you can increase your price as you go.
- *Explain why your bid is low.* You don't need to tell the client that you are learning, but you might want to say that you are bidding low in order to get your first reviews on this site. They will see that you have no reviews, and referring to it yourself will show that you understand their concern and have made a low bid as a result.
- *Don't take on big jobs.* You're still learning, so avoid big or technically advanced jobs. Feel free to take on jobs slightly above your current skill level, as long as you're confident you can learn what will be required, but the last thing you want is a bad review and a disgruntled client.
- *Clarify the job.* It's essential that you're clear on what is required, and that it has been objectively stated on the freelance site messaging system. That way, if there is any

disagreement, you can refer back to what the job was originally set out to be. Ambiguous language or general aims (such as 'build me a site') are a recipe for disaster.

- *Agree on payment structure.* Even with small projects, it's important to make it clear when payment will be due. We would advise not to start work until a milestone is created (ie the buyer has made a downpayment, which is held by the freelancer site until the job is finished). That way, if there are any disagreements, it is up to the freelancer site to establish whether the work has been done and release the payment.
- *Be wary of buyers with no reviews.* Buyers have reviews too, and if a buyer has no reviews, be careful. They may well be reliable, but they may not be – in this case it is particularly important to make sure the requirements of the job are clear, and that a milestone is paid before you start work.

Why not get started now? Take a couple of hours and create a profile on the freelance site of your choice. Start bidding on simple projects, making sure to keep your price low and your communication fast and clear. We wouldn't be surprised if you had your first gig by the end of the day. Good luck!

Building a portfolio

As a developer, your portfolio website will likely be more important than your CV. Your site should make clear what your strengths are as a developer, and showcase some of your best work. It should make potential clients and employers excited to work with you.

Your website should reflect your style and personality, so if possible create it from scratch. If you prefer, however, there are a range of Wordpress themes that you can use to create a great-looking portfolio quickly. It is important that your portfolio site looks good, so we would advise spending $50 or so on a theme from templatemonster.com or https://themeforest.net/. They both have Wordpress portfolio sections at https://themeforest.net/category/

wordpress/creative/portfolio and www.templatemonster.com/ portfolio-wordpress-themes.

Take some time to browse some of the best developers' portfolio sites, and include their best features. Project Stories are particularly useful to potential clients and employers. In a Project Story you explain the clients' needs, how you met them, and what technologies you used to achieve their goals. Combined with a screenshot or a link to the project itself, and a testimonial from the client, this can be a very powerful way to show your level of experience and competence, as well as your ability to explain your work clearly.

Take time over your portfolio site, and make sure there is room to expand it as you learn new skills and complete new projects. It will hopefully be your standard bearer for many years to come, so it's worth getting it right.

Expanding your online presence

It is very likely that potential employers will search your name on Google, so it is important that your online presence is cohesive and impressive. We have talked at length about having a blog, and also tending to your Twitter feed and portfolio. But there are other things you can do to boost your online image.

Keep your LinkedIn profile up to date

LinkedIn is by far the biggest professional social network. You should have a LinkedIn page, and it should reflect the jobs you are applying for. So all the above advice applies: express your experience and roles concisely and keep everything up to date. Include links to the projects you have worked on and testimonials.

Have a GitHub page

GitHub is a very popular site for storing code, usually for open source applications. If you build tools, such as a JavaScript image slider, or simple apps such as an iPhone calculator, put them on your GitHub page. Not only will it help other people but it will give you another place to show your talents and experience.

You might also want to consider contributing to open source projects. Anyone can do this, and it is a great way to give back to the community that likely produced a lot of the free tools you have used so far to build websites and apps. However, you need to be sure that you know what you are doing if you contribute to projects – contributing poorly written or buggy code will not make you any friends within the community.

Writing a software developer CV

The process of writing a CV for a software developer is much the same as for other industries: keep it concise, honest, relevant and don't belittle your achievements. If you are looking at a career change into coding, you might be wondering how much of your previous work to include, and how to 'talk up' your relative lack of development experience.

Our advice would be to include each of your roles (ideally leave no gaps in your timeline), but don't go into detail of what the work involved. If you want to get work as a developer, you should focus on what you have done to develop your new skills, and the portfolio of work you have developed. As with your portfolio, clarify what particular languages and environments you are familiar with, as evidenced by the projects you have worked on.

It is likely that some people that read your CV will not be technical, and will instead be looking for keywords such as

JavaScript or PHP, so make sure you include all relevant skill areas explicitly. The word 'relevant' there is important – be aware of the job you are applying for and tailor your list of skills accordingly. A complete laundry list of every language you've ever worked with is not required!

A great technique here is to state what you like and dislike about the tools you have used – this shows that you understand them well enough to be familiar with their foibles. You can do this in a 'summary' section, which also includes a statement about your overall level of experience, and also some of the personal projects you have worked on. This will show that you have a genuine interest in programming, and also give you something interesting to talk about in the interview.

As always, be honest – don't claim to have years of coding experience if you don't, but do make clear that you are a fast learner and you have achieved a lot in the short time you have been coding. If you are applying for appropriate jobs (ie entry-level coding positions), your employer won't expect a huge amount of experience or a degree in computer science, but they will want to see that you have the basic technical skills they are looking for, and that you are genuinely interested in what you do.

The interview

As with CVs, all the standard interview advice applies here: be personable and interested in your interviewers, and have a strong knowledge of the company and the role you are applying for. As well as this, read your CV thoroughly and write down at least 20 questions that you might be asked about what you've written (if you can't think of 20, ask a friend or family member). Write down great answers to these questions, and read them out loud several times. This will help you give confident, fluent answers to questions that are bound to come your way.

Your interviewers will likely be a technical manager (your future boss), fellow coders (your future colleagues) and possibly a non-technical HR representative. Imagine the interview from their perspective – they would likely rather be doing something else, so try to be upbeat and enthusiastic, and talk confidently about the interesting side projects you mentioned on your CV.

Keeping up to date with industry news is also a great way to show that you are genuinely interested in programming, and gives you something of substance to talk about instead of small talk.

Summary

The process described in this chapter – that of building a portfolio, working on freelance jobs, writing your CV and attending interviews, to finally landing a programming job is not a quick one. You should allow at least a year. But remember you'll learn a huge amount along the way, and gain technical and personal skills that will be useful regardless of whether you become a full-time developer or not.

Conclusion

Congratulations – you've made it through this book. Along the way you've hopefully picked up some knowledge and insight into the world of coding and skills which will stand you in good stead wherever your career path may take you. Wherever you decide to take your new-found skills we would urge you to expand and learn more. Actively seek out and find coding opportunities. Identify those potential projects in your existing workplace or indeed realize that entrepreneurial idea that has been on the back burner all these years. Your objective is to construct a reason, a requirement, perhaps even a business mandate for you to put your learning into practice and build experience. After all, necessity is the mother of all invention.

So what now? In the latter chapters of this book we outlined several opportunities that learning code brings you. We hope that you have already started taking on some of these opportunities, but just in case, let us now briefly recap some of the primary next steps. You should aim to choose between two and five of these to ensure that your development continues, and that you get the most out of reading this book.

Work better

Consider several ways in which you could work more efficiently utilizing the technologies that we have covered. Think about burdensome, typically administrative tasks in your workplace that through application of your technical skills you could in some way automate and thus save significant time for your colleagues.

Using your coding skills to work more effectively is a great way to provide additional value for your employer and your customers, which inevitably benefits you as you gain recognition for your endeavours delivering these improvements to the business.

Build a website or app

With even limited initial skills you can quickly start to produce sites and apps which are small tools to answer particular business needs. As well as naturally advancing your skills and experience, looking for opportunities involving small discrete apps and services will enhance the breadth and depth of your portfolio. You will be surprised how even limited applications, successfully delivered and serving a client, will quickly result in further follow-on work and expanded feature requests from the client.

These websites and apps don't always need to fulfil a specific business objective or have initial remuneration. For instance, you might identify a need for a community web space for a local initiative or an effective solution in your own workspace which saves you and perhaps your team significant time with processes.

Become an entrepreneur

Coding skills are unrivalled in their capacity to allow you to begin your own business venture. We have already looked at formulating your idea and establishing whether there is a demand for it. Remember that even the genius that is Mark Zuckerberg began his project in a college dormitory as a basic picture rating application. His real brilliance was in realizing the potential for his idea and adapting his approach to meet the demand for his application and its services. Have a bigger picture in your mind, but start off small, manageable and achievable and build up from there. You'd be really surprised at how effective rapid prototyping of smaller concepts is at expanding and breeding new ideas.

Don't be afraid to step into territory that is already served by applications and or websites. Those incumbent services may not be performing as well as they could or perhaps alternatively you may have identified a niche offering within that sector.

Become a developer

If you are considering a full-time career change then you are on to a winner. As we have already discussed, coding is one of the few unique professions that are truly global. Provided you can demonstrate skill and competence in your chosen technologies, then the world is your oyster. Suddenly visa restrictions are relaxed, your transferable and greatly in-demand skills are valuable, tradable commodities allowing you to negotiate favourable working conditions and remuneration at relatively high levels. Better still, as long as you keep abreast of changing technologies, maintain and update your portfolio and master new skills then there is very little risk of your chosen career leading to redundancy. The trajectory of demand for IT workers is continually upwards and I predict it will increase exponentially in the not-so-distant future.

Learn more

Once you have mastered the basics, perhaps the single most important thing to do is to start to put theory into practice. Complement the theory component with practical applications, much like we have done in this book. This process is a powerful learning technique forcing the brain and memory to commit and retrieve information. Our minds are powerful devices, but they are organized around context. As an exercise, try to picture your best friend from primary school or your beloved pet when you were a child. It is difficult. If you now try with a context – think of a special memory or occasion – suddenly they appear a lot more clearly in your thoughts and you start to recall much more detail.

In addition to your portfolio, try to seek out active challenges and build specifications for a technical solution around those. Those challenges will naturally include additional elements or unique scenarios which will push the envelope of your learning and enhance your skills. Much like when you learn a new spoken language the key is to actively engage in situations which force you to apply and adapt your learning to the situation. If I was to ask the market trader in Barcelona for two apples in my best Spanish, they might well respond with a clarification of whether I would like green or red apples or one of each for example.

It would be amazing if reading this book alone would make you the complete coder, but clearly it is just the start of your journey. You will want to further your learning by accessing books and online courses. Years of collective teaching experience have taught me and Rob that presenting material from as many view-points as possible is a sure-fire way to cement student learning. Read as much and from as many sources as you can to firm up your understanding.

A few suggestions are given below. They are by no means exhaustive and there are lots of good resources out there:

- O'Reilly, Apress – publishers of a very large range of technical books authored by experts in the topics covered.
- Udemy.com – a huge range of courses across all topics.
- Pluralsight.com – again, a huge library of courses but with a specific focus on just IT and relevant learning pathways.
- Codecademy.com – interactive coding courses, many free, on web development and related courses.

To bring this book to a close let us remember that it's about knowledge, the ability to understand how something may be accomplished rather than knowing the full syntax of a particular solution or implementation. The modern-day advantage of liter-ally millions of coding samples, implementation and support networks online means that you are never far from a specific answer or indeed friendly assistance from support sites and forums.

Learn and experience as much as you can across different technologies to equip you to surmount any challenge with confidence, efficiency and flexibility. Identify and scope the specific technical challenges within the solution. Always remember the adage that '20% of the problem is 80% of the work', and so if you break the back of that 20% at the outset then you are flying.

Approach problems and challenges with enthusiasm and verve and, much like we did as children, break them down into smaller discrete problems. Suddenly the most imposing conun-drums become logical steps along a path to success. Don't be afraid to go for the big technical hurdle first.

To whimsically meander back through our narrative to the original scrawled graffiti on that windswept, dreary grey train platform:

"If not now, when?"

And to finally ask... what exactly are you waiting for?

Index

9 781398 611887